Simple Changes

§

Quietly Overcoming Barriers
to Personal and Professional Growth

Also by Robert J. Wicks . . .

Sharing Wisdom

Everyday Simplicity

Living a Gentle, Passionate Life

Companions in Hope (with Thomas Rodgerson)

After 50

A Circle of Friends (with Robert Hamma)

Seeds of Sensitivity

Touching the Holy

Seeking Perspective

Living Simply in an Anxious World

Availability: The Spiritual Joy of Helping Others

Simple Changes

§

*Quietly Overcoming Barriers
to Personal and Professional Growth*

Robert J. Wicks

Ways to discover new freedom in your life
through a gentle, step-by-step approach to
integrating contemporary psychology
with classic spiritual wisdom

ThomasMore®
– An RCL Company –

Allen, Texas

Acknowledgments

I am grateful to John Sprague, Publisher of Thomas More, for his encouragement at each step of the development of this book. Thanks also goes to Karyn Felder for typing draft after draft until it was "just right." Finally, my appreciation (as always) to my wife Michaele for her inspiration, editing, and generous spirit. The "small changes" for the good I have made in my life have found faithful support in her.

Send all inquiries to: THOMAS MORE PUBLISHING
An RCL Company
200 East Bethany Drive
Allen, Texas 75002-3804

Web site: www.RCLweb.com

E-mail: cservice@rcl-enterprises.com

Telephone: 877-275-4725 / 972-390-6300

Fax: 800-688-8356 / 972-390-6560

Printed in the United States of America

Library of Congress Catalog Card Number 00133318

ISBN 0-88347-462-X

1 2 3 4 5   04 03 02 01 00

Dedication

For Jim Barker,
a compassionate presence in
so many lives . . . including my own

When you are fooled by something else, the damage will not be so big. But when you are fooled by yourself, it is fatal. No more medicine. [1]

Shunryu Suzuki

All day I have been uncomfortably aware of the wrong that is in me. The useless burden of pride I condemn myself to carry, and all that comes with carrying it. I know I deceive myself . . . but I cannot catch myself in the act. I do not see exactly where the deception lies. [2]

Thomas Merton

Every patient stared at long enough, listened to hard enough, yields up a child arrived at from somewhere else, caught up in a confused life, trying to do the right thing, whatever that might be, and doing the wrong thing instead. [3]

Robert F. Rodman

Table of Contents

Motivation Is Not Enough:
Taking Simple Steps to Encourage
  Inner Freedom   **9**

I

*Quietly Planting Seeds of Inner Freedom,
Growth and Change*

1. Making Space Within   **19**

2. Sweet Disgust   **25**

3. Wonderful Negative Experiences
     and Worries   **31**

4. Personal Intrigue!   **35**

5. Bring the Responsibilities Home   **39**

6. Change Begins in Front of You   **43**

7. Making Time to Change   **47**

8. Your Private Place   **51**

9. Real Preparation for Change   **57**

10. What Have We Got?   **61**

11. Pacing   **67**

12. Letting Go   **69**

13. Bringing Role Models Closer   **75**

14. More Helpful Voices   **81**

15. Real Generosity   **85**

16. A Little Effort   **89**

II

So What Else Would You Like to
    Know about Resolving Psychological
    Resistances to Growth and Change?   **95**

How to Defeat Yourself Effectively
    and Make Yourself Miserable
    No Matter How Good Your Life Is   **101**

III

Dialogue with the Sages:
Spiritual Approaches to "Softening the Soul"   **109**

A Question of Inner Freedom: An Epilogue   **125**

Appendix I—A Month of Change:
    An At-Home 30-Day Retreat   **131**

Appendix II—Some Helpful Books   **141**

Motivation Is Not Enough

Taking Simple Steps to Encourage *Inner Freedom*

In the early years of psychology, a client's resistance to change was often looked upon as solely a *motivational* problem. When a person did not succeed in changing, the counselor felt: "I did my job in pointing out your difficulties. In return, you didn't do yours!" The blame rested upon the one seeking change. The goal was to eliminate the resistances and get the person motivated again.

Now, we recognize that when someone resists change and growth in their personal and professional lives they are not purposely giving family, friends, coworkers and counselors a hard time. Instead, they are unconsciously providing a great deal of critical information on problematic areas of their life given their personality style, history, and current situation. This material then becomes a real source of new wisdom for psychological growth, professional advancement, and spiritual insight.

Though we still believe motivation is an essential key to making progress, we see that persons seeking change must also gain certain knowledge about themselves and act on it if they wish to advance. Or in a nutshell: *Motivation or positive thinking is good, but it is obviously not enough.*

In other words: If you fall off a horse, you should get right back on. And, if you fall off again, you should get right back on again and again. This is true. But it would make things easier if you also took a few riding lessons!

That's what *Simple Changes* is all about. It is a little introduction on how to learn from, embrace, and ride with, on, around, and through the natural resistances everyone must encounter in their personal, spiritual, and professional lives. No one is ever without some obvious or hidden blocks to growth, change, and *inner freedom*.

At times, experiencing resistances within ourselves can be annoying, puzzling, or frustrating, since most of us really do want to advance and deepen as persons. Yet while we may be upset, there is no need to give up. Now with just a bit of effort and direction there is so much we can do to make life more meaningful and worthwhile. Positive change and greater inner freedom need not require a dramatic program. Instead it can occur gradually, *quietly*. Oftentimes we just need a little helpful information and guidance.

The field of contemporary psychology and psychiatry as well as the classic spiritual wisdom literature presently available offer us a wealth of information on why people have a hard time changing and what to do to enable progress to occur. However, much of this information is not readily accessible. Thus, the real challenge is how to find and explore this helpful material in order to take the simple steps that encourage greater inner freedom.

The psychological information on overcoming resistance in the professional literature for therapists is not generally available to the public. Similarly, the spiritual wisdom on facing blocks in life is often embedded in the classic religious literature of each faith tradition. As such, it is sometimes difficult to read and apply in light of today's challenges. Also, it may not be easy to find even if you are a member of that faith community.

Another difficulty in benefiting from spiritual wisdom is the paucity of interreligious dialogue. Spiritual wisdom of one religious tradition is often inaccessible or outside the experience of those from other faith traditions. For instance, the average Catholic would probably not read Ram Dass and a devout Buddhist might not think to reflect on the words of Father Anthony de Mello, a Jesuit priest. Yet paradoxically, both could benefit and advance personally, professionally, and even spiritually in their *own* faith if they did. You don't need to see spirituality as a smorgasbord or be a "spiritual tourist" to appreciate how the wisdom of other faiths can be nurturing to your own beliefs and psychology of living.

For over twenty years I have sought to find and employ the most powerful and practical psychological and spiritual methods to overcome resistance to change and facilitate growth among one of the most sophisticated (and sometimes surprisingly inordinately resistant) populations: members of the helping and healing professions. Psychotherapists, ministers, relief workers, nurses and physicians, educators, and spiritual leaders are responsible for the welfare of others. Given this, when they themselves seek help, unless the guidance is clear, practical, and able to show proven results, their response is quick and direct and sounds something like this: "I know the approach you have just described is good standard practice. In fact, I suggest it myself to others. But it won't work with *me*."

Nevertheless, good, simple, and powerful approaches do work with them and will work with me and you if we apply them in a gradual, careful, and persistent fashion. Our resistances to change are no match for true psychological and spiritual wisdom. If we expend even a little effort we will see that change, while not easy, is simple and the first step is a commitment to wake up to how we are blocking ourselves from so much more in life. As one spiritual guide wryly reminds us:

> *To a man who hesitated to embark*
>
> *on the spiritual quest for fear of the*
>
> *effort and renunciation the Master said:*
>
> *"How much effort and renunciation*
>
> *does it take to open one's eyes and see?"* [4]

The same lesson applies to persons in business, education, ministry . . . in fact, to *all* of us in life. But, once again, motivation is not enough. We must know how to face resistances to change. For instance, at times we may even need to go around them rather than take them on directly. A frontal assault will not work.

Zen monks, for example, found that children who endured the horrors of war often manifested the classic signs of trauma: distrust, an exaggerated startle reaction, fear of betrayal, a loss of personal security, and an inability to experience joy. And, if the monks tried to handle these problems directly with the children they would fail. So instead they decided to plant healing seeds in their unconscious next to the hurts, hoping they would grow, take root in the inner life, and in turn indirectly heal the hurts. To do this they smiled at the children, played with them, taught and ate warm meals with them. Slowly, in return, the traumatic glassy look in their eyes faded and their faces and souls came to life again in joy.

Simple Steps to Encourage Greater *Inner Freedom*

Like the Zen monks just described, *Simple Changes* will plant similar seeds of new freedom, growth, and change. Like "little sound bytes" on television, each chapter will only take a few minutes to read before you start your busy day. My suggestion is that you take another few minutes to reflect on the words you have read sometime during the day. Finally, spend a minute or so on the theme of the chapter you read earlier just before going to bed to further seed the idea in your heart.

After reviewing the brief chapters provided, I think you will be pleased at how some of the resistances to necessary change you thought would never lessen are "melted" by your own thoughts and commitment to living a deeper, richer life. Absorbing sound psychological and spiritual wisdom will enable this to happen in a gentle, step-by-step fashion. Dramatic resolutions or fad "self-improvement" diets don't work. In the end they just discourage us from believing real change is both possible and enjoyable. On the other hand, a quiet, developmental approach to behavioral and attitudinal change that "loosens our psyche up" and "softens our soul" so we can be more open, can be very powerful.

Following the "seeds of change" there is a second section on commonly asked questions about resolving psychological resistances to growth and change, a third section on questions often asked of spiritual guides on how to be open, and an epilogue. Finally, there are two appendices: an at-home thirty-day retreat encouraging openness to change and a brief descriptive bibliography. The appendices have been included to round out the information on how to logically understand and carefully overcome resistances to change.

To emphasize once again: With what we now know about resistance from psychology and about increasing our awareness from spirituality, there are many basic steps we can take to get more out of our personal and professional lives. Certainly, given the preciousness and fleeting nature of life, isn't it worth the effort to expend some energy in this direction each day?

May the words that follow help you to relax, be more flexible, and grow, as you journey toward finding greater meaning and freedom in life. Let this book help you enjoy life *while* you are changing—don't wait until you reach your goals. Personal growth need not be a chore, but rather a continually surprising journey to explore and love.

Robert J. Wicks
Loyola College in Maryland

*Face reality and effortless
change will take place.*

~ Zen saying

*The one who would be consistent
in happiness must frequently change.*

~ Confucius

I

Quietly Planting Inner Seeds of Freedom,
Growth, and Change

1. Making Space Within

By questioning further

One of the most precious graces of life is freedom, *inner* freedom. To change, move, *really* grow, we need "space" within ourselves. Habits, worries, emotions, defensiveness, stubbornness, and fear all take up room. Maybe that's why Zen Roshis suggests that to find joy and peace, we don't need to *add* something to our lives. Instead, we need to *drop* something so we can see clearly and live more freely. From a Christian vantage point, this is called "purity of heart." Psychologists are less poetic. They simply suggest: Get rid of "expensive defenses" that take up all your energy. Their suggestion: Uncover and eliminate old, useless habits and unfounded, erroneous, negative beliefs, and the result will be new freedom.

However, while the goal (namely, having space, emptiness, or freedom within) sounds good, it is not easy. Why? Because the first step goes completely against the grain of our "common sense" and presently limited self-awareness. To be free, we must first realize that in many ways, we are not!

There are all types of hidden addictions, ingrained habits, and unexamined beliefs that are guiding us automatically through life. One of the best ways to find out what they are is to continually monitor our emotions and ask the right type of questions that eventually lead to information that frees us.

Self-awareness and sensitivity to what we "fill our psyches with" seems so elusive. I think Thoreau was right when he said "It is as hard to see oneself as it is to look backward without turning 'round.'" Much of my work is with a "professionally sensitive" population. These "healers" and helpers generally consider themselves in tune with themselves and their environment because of their work and professional roles. Yet those who are truly sensitive are the ones who seek to learn new lessons and "unlearn" old habits each day.

To be aware like that we must have a questioning air that is fueled by an appreciation of our emotions. In other words, we need to be able and willing to be sensitive to what our emotions can teach us. When we are angry, sad, thrilled, anxious, fearful, or depressed, we are tempted to think the emotion is being caused by some external event in our lives. That is only partly true. The interpretation we attach to the event plays the major role in eliciting a given emotion.

For example, we might have a friend who asks for recommendations for books to read or movies to view. Then he calls to criticize the choices. ("The plot is not well-developed." "The ending is not believable." "The humor was lagging.")

Our first reaction might be: "Well, why do you ask me for suggestions if you are always going to play the critic?" At work when someone asks for ideas and then repeatedly rejects them, we may ask a similar question: "Why did you ask if you are only going to reject them (and try to make me feel inferior in the process)?"

You may also ask yourself: "Why is he so critical? Doesn't he know I am going to get tired of it and stop offering suggestions?" The answer to this is quite simply: No, he probably doesn't see himself as being critical. Also, in this style of behavior he may unconsciously feel he will impress you with his own knowledge even though it is off-putting. The reason behind it may be that it is more important for him to feel superior than to have your friendship, for if he valued it, he would be more gentle and sensitive. Fear, which underlies insecurity and neediness, often causes such behavior.

Still, now that we have gone on this "psychoanalytic safari" and analyzed why he behaves in this irritating fashion, what have we got that will make more space in our life? Nothing really. We may decide either not to suggest anything in the future or just expect he will rarely be happy with our recommendations. But even though we may have made our life a little more pleasant by the decision, we still haven't opened up any more space in our inner life to change or grow, we haven't yet asked the right type of question. We haven't questioned far enough.

We always ask questions about the other person(s) or event(s) that are precipitating emotions in our lives. This is a natural response. In the case just cited, it is normal to ask: What is the matter with him? Why does he behave in such a critical fashion? Doesn't he realize he just pushes potential friends away by being so dissatisfied with suggestions (gifts) offered to him?

However, after these outer-directed questions are asked and our emotions of anger or annoyance dissipate a bit, then it is time to ask really useful questions: Why did *I* allow myself to be so upset over someone else's behavior? Given my reactions, what can I learn about my own insecurities and agendas that will make me more self-aware, less defensive . . . more *free?* Such a change in the focus and extent of our questioning helps us retrieve the power to alter our future reactions.

Knowing the answers to such questions clears our inner space. If we don't ask these questions or if we stop in the questioning process too soon, we only uncover information that is useful for the other persons but not for ourselves. And the sad part is that it probably won't be useful to them either. Since their behavior is unconsciously motivated or is tied to an unexamined belief about themselves and their world they would naturally deny our interpretation even if we offered it to them on a silver platter. Besides, when we are annoyed by another's behavior, we are probably the last person able to help them. In such cases, our motivations to help would be less than pure and our response would more than likely be aimed at paying them back or showing them how they injured us rather than for their benefit.

Yet in irritating and other unpleasant situations we can help ourselves by tilling the psychological and spiritual soil, and planting new self-knowledge that will lead to opportunities for necessary growth and change. Wouldn't that be a better option than just moodily focusing on the silly behavior of others and our own hurt feelings? Wouldn't it be better to reclaim the power we are wasting in interpersonal situations so as to alter our reaction style both interiorly and interpersonally? How we question ourselves—especially when annoyed, hurt, or experiencing a negative emotion—is an important key to self-understanding, changing destructive patterns of reactions, and making space within for new learning opportunities.

Seed of Change #1

After reflecting on why someone with whom you interact behaves the way he (she) does, ask why you are reacting the way you are. In this way, you can gain further insight into your own defenses, needs, insecurities, and blind areas. Change needs the room occupied by these defenses. Make space within yourself by psychologically and spiritually "cleaning out" your inner life.

2. Sweet Disgust

When being fed up is good

In therapy one of the main reasons people are willing to attempt a program of change is that they are thoroughly fed up with their lives. Such a situation offers a favorable time to risk new attitudes, perceptions, and behaviors in lieu of the status quo. The same holds true for the spiritual life. People come to Hindu swamis, Buddhist rinpoches, Christian mystics, Taoist sages, or Jewish rebbes with the wish to live life differently, with more meaning, and a greater sense of the holy at the center of their lives.

Whether you call it sin, ingrained habits, unexamined erroneous beliefs, or early life experiences which have led to crippling transferences, people at this juncture want to both see and experience life differently. They want to *change*.

As the interaction proceeds, the therapist or guru realizes that what is *really* being asked though is: *Can I change without really changing? Can I alter only those parts of my life which are causing me pain but essentially remain as I am? Or, more to the point, can I have relief but no real cure that will require me to work to significantly alter my style, perception, or beliefs?*

This basic resistance to change is natural and to be expected in others and ourselves. Whenever we look at a challenge or problem, we must first and foremost include ourselves in the examination. However, people are trained to be economical in their energy with respect to self-examination and self-change. The preference is to look outward. And so, when the situation gets so bad that they want to be off the treadmill of worries, no longer strapped to the wheel of *suffering*, and really feel they are disgusted with the way they are living their lives, this is a wonderful opportunity to make a move to increase self-awareness and enable profound change.

When our attitude and outlook change, our perspective on the whole world around us is altered as well. If a poor man is grateful, his watery soup is much tastier than a wealthy man's fine meal. Furthermore, a person who is happy inside will more often look with a sense of wonder at those around him.

That is why spending time looking in disgust at the negative patterns in our lives, as part of our daily reflection, need not be an exercise in masochism. It can be a step forward in enlightenment! If this is so, then why don't we do it? Why don't we look at the compulsion, anger, greed, narcissism, and stress in our life directly and honestly?

Well, I think we fear seeing the truth and we worry what such insight might demand of us—namely, that we would have to:

§ *See our own role in making our life a painful web of grasping demands, insecurities, anger, envy, and resentment, and do something about it;*

§ *Become more aware of the time we have lost behaving in a way that has been nonproductive and frozen because we have projected blame outward as an excuse for not doing something inward;*

§ *Face the other's reaction to our new movement toward freedom, love, and peace and away from competition, defensiveness, and inauthenticity. The reality is while other people say they want us to grow and change, they often feel quite uncomfortable when we do.*

Still, despite our hesitation, being fed up with our current ways of perceiving and coping can encourage us toward needed change. Seeing again and again the negative results of our thinking, feeling, and behaving can push us to say, "Enough! I don't want to live this way anymore!" That's a great motivation to begin change. Staying with it is another story.

In therapy, when people start to get better they are tempted to take a "leap into health" and stop their program of change. In response, the therapist seeks to help them continue to challenge themselves so their overall attitude is changed. Spiritual guidance uses a similar approach. When a disciple achieves *kensho* (an awakening), the guide allows him to enjoy the experience. However, he/she also cautions the seeker to move on, not make the experience into an idol. The disciple is encouraged to seek *dai kensho*, a complete breakdown of the walls of habit and illusion so life can be seen and experienced for what it is: simple, beautiful reality.

A psychospiritual program of change requires no less. It seeks to help us see the distress in our lives as a function of our holding on to old beliefs, hurts, expectations, needs, perceptions, and angers. It wants us to never forget the personal expense of holding onto the narrow views that manage our lives according to a set approach at the cost of fully enjoying it.

So, one of the very things that encourages psychology clients and spiritual seekers to stay the course to greater inner freedom is the one which must be practiced by all people who wish to be open to profound change: the willingness and ability to look directly at life's painful experiences in order to learn from them rather than bumping into the same wall again and again. Several simple examples of this are:

> *Interpersonally,* **needy** *persons need to look directly at the negative results of being too overbearing in their relationships. They need to see the impact of their behavior again and again until they are so disgusted they don't want to do that again.*

> **Greedy** *individuals need to see that their avarice (i.e., in regard to the stock market) can and has resulted in losing the very thing they wanted—newfound wealth;*

> **Insecure** *individuals need to see that many of the actions they take to produce security actually result in greater instability because appropriate personal, vocational, financial, and interpersonal risks were not taken.*

And, we need to recognize that we are like all of the above people in some way. This is why we must recognize our pain, cease behaving in ways that encourage it, and take responsibility not to walk into the same wall again and again, while complaining that the wall shouldn't be there!

In order to accomplish change in the most annoying parts of our lives we need to ask:

§ *Why is this really annoying to me?*

§ *How am I making this so troublesome for me (and of great importance)?*

§ *What can I do about it?*

By asking and answering these three questions again and again, the wall of resistance melts, making change and real freedom a real possibility.

Seed of Change #2

"Sweet disgust" which enables us to see our own role in making our life a painful web of grasping demands, insecurities, anger, envy, and resentment should not lead to self-condemnation. Instead, it should inspire us to take small steps each day to understand our reaction so we can put this insight into a practical response.

3. *Wonderful Negative Experiences and Worries*

Or, how to be more objective and stand on, rather
than be bothered by, the irritating things
and persons in your life

When lecturing in Japan, I had an opportunity to visit one of their holiest Shinto Shrines, *Ise Jingo*. During this visit I was given a personal tour of the temple grounds by one of its directors, a former woodsman, who had a real feeling for animism which is the source of this ancient religion.

As we were crossing a beautiful arching wooden bridge, he stopped, looked down, pointed, and said: "What do you see?" Not quite sure of what he was looking for from me, I nonetheless calmly replied in the best way I could: "Calm, clear water."

He smiled and replied: "Hai" (yes) and went on to ask: "Now, what do you hear?" To which I said: "A frog." In response he nodded again and said: "You will not hear this species of frog anywhere else on the temple grounds."

"Why?" I asked.

Then he looked directly at me with his large, deep brown eyes and said: "Because this species of frog lives only near water that is fresh, clear, and at peace."[5]

Later, as I reflected on this interaction, I realized we weren't really speaking about frogs and water. Instead, I was being taught by this gentleman about what I could experience in life if my heart was at peace and my mind clear. Meditation and simple quiet time alone offer this kind of possibility. It is easy to have such time when we simply slow ourselves down, sit up straight with our hands resting in front of us on our lap, breathe easily through our nose, and keep a "light alertness" to the in-and-out movements of our breath.

During such quiet moments which take no advanced training, we settle down, stop rushing around doing things, and open ourselves to greater awareness and peace. Wonderful, right? Well, in keeping with the persistence of inner resistance to growth and change, not quite.

Many people avoid such quiet time because in meditation or during such periods of silence and solitude not only do we eventually experience ourselves at rest which is beneficial physiologically, psychologically, and spiritually, but we also initially see some things we may not like but which we have hidden even from ourselves.

These hidden worries may include the games we play interpersonally at work, the anxieties and insecurities about our personal life, or the sense that in so many ways we are charlatans (i.e., "If people only knew what we were really like!"). The fact that this happens is not terrible. It only feels that way initially because the image we have created of ourselves is temporarily under attack. As a matter of fact, it is actually good because the only negative perception we have of ourselves that can harm us is the one about which we are not aware.

If we remain seated, hold the reality of our unique gifted presence in this world deep in our mind and heart, and nonjudgmentally view these perceptions and worries like a train passing through the station, we will find out a great deal of helpful information about what is undermining us and causing inadvertent resistance to growth and change. (You know the old saying: "I have met the enemy and it is *I*.")

You may even see that things you believe about yourself deep down are false. You know they are because in your daily reactions you may have verbally defended yourself when you felt accused of them.

For instance, an executive may constantly bristle if she feels she's not being treated with respect. Yet in meditation she may see that because she wasn't taken seriously in her family, she has on occasion actually behaved like a child at work, then was annoyed when people spotted this immature style of behavior and called her on it—possibly in a teasing way, which in some ways is worse because it prolongs the problem.

A wealth of information is available to us each day when we quiet ourselves down for a few moments. Quiet time and reflection can be tremendously helpful if:

1. *We are careful to avoid either projecting the blame onto others for a negative encounter or condemning ourselves;*

2. *We look nonjudgmentally at the worries about the day's experience to see what we can learn from them; and*

3. *We write our reflections down after the quiet period is up so we can think further about them and later discuss them with a trusted friend, colleague, or mentor.*

Seed of Change #3

Negative experiences and hidden worries can be sources of help when they become conscious, are viewed nonjudgmentally, and are examined with an eye to see how they can profitably direct our energies to develop and change.

4. *Personal Intrigue!*

Not arrogance or ignorance

The two greatest enemies of growth and change are *arrogance* and *ignorance*. These two extremes waste more energy than any other defensive maneuver. In fact, if we avoided both of them, growth would happen almost spontaneously and naturally. Zen Buddhists have a great proverb that illustrates this: "Face reality and effortless change will take place."

Arrogance occurs when we export (project) the responsibility for our failures and mistakes. The words that reflect that this process is going on are:

§ *Projection*

§ *Blaming*

§ *Excusing*

§ *Absolving*

§ *Exploring*

§ *Rationalizing*

§ *Mitigating*

§ *Contextualizing*

The more subtle the words and sophisticated our excuses, the more we hide the following central truth from ourselves: *We* have a primary role in removing the blocks to growth and change.

At the other end of the spectrum is *ignorance*. This occurs when we take all of the responsibility for failure in a way that results in our feeling negative about ourselves. Such self-debasement does not lead to insight or personal responsibility. Instead, it only ends in feeling guilty, shameful, or seeing ourselves as failures.

Also, since behavior that we wince at turns into behavior that we wink at, such self-blame eventually burns itself out. So, we feel overwhelmed rather than empowered, discouraged rather than enlightened, and we avoid further understanding rather than delve deeper for information that will set us free.

Some of the ways we describe this process are:

§ *Self-condemnation*

§ *Over-responsibility*

§ *Being hypercritical of self*

§ *Overly perfectionistic tendencies*

As a positive alternative therapists encourage their patients to be *intrigued* by their behavior. They want them to be detectives who explore the mystery of the self. Spiritual guides offer the same encouragement. Buddhists, for instance, recommend that people watch themselves objectively—neither condemning nor excusing so they can see their own grasping tendencies and the evil results such attitudes cause.

Mentors of all sorts often tease people to get them to realize how overly serious they are about their mistakes.

In response to a person condemning themselves, the comment may be: "I don't think anyone in the state has ever made such a creative mistake before!" Breaking up the tension to understand the dynamics, rather than be involved in rumination, is an essential part of intrigue.

Furthermore, at the other end of the spectrum, projection of blame onto others is discouraged as well: "If the source of the problem resides fully in the world outside of us, then we will have to change everyone else for it to improve. Quite a job for us!"

When we give away the blame, we also give away the power to change. But if we neutrally look at our own role with a sense of intrigue, not self-condemnation, we can increase the power that is within us. This takes practice. Accordingly, I suggest people go through several steps to encourage intrigue:

1. *Anytime you have a strong feeling about something, immediately act as if it is someone else experiencing the feeling;*

2. *Observe any temptation to blame others or condemn oneself;*

3. *Be a detective who is awed by the subtle temptations to be arrogant/ignorant and get intrigued by the whole process to the point where one is excited about uncovering the mystery of the real cause of the problem.*

Seed of Change #4

Be aware that the two greatest enemies of inner freedom, growth, and change are arrogance (projecting the blame for our failure onto others) and ignorance (self-condemnation). Instead, the source of psychological and spiritual freedom is intrigue about the mystery and movement of our life.

5. Bring the Responsibilities Home

Not with vindictiveness but with love, as you would a prodigal child

Clarity is the medium of both new freedom and the ability to change. Many people never gain this state because they view the challenges and questions in their life without including the most important factor: *themselves*. Knowing and loving ourselves allows us to be more objective in how we see things. Ignorance, fear, and dislike of self cause our vision to be murky. At times we are so filled with emotion, rationalization, and denial of the realities involved that we are completely blind. No matter. If we understand this, then we can begin to open our psychological and spiritual eyes and see again. Once we do that we can stand on our own two feet and walk toward our next goal while fully enjoying and learning from the trip itself. Nothing, no pain or failure, is wasted.

So what will enhance the possibility that we will be more and more honest with ourselves? The answer is that whatever would increase the chances for others to accept questions and feedback from us are the same factors that would increase our own willingness to embrace self-understanding. Included among them are: style of approach, awareness of the positive, toughness, willingness to deal with unpleasant specifics, and need for action based on insight.

Style of approach with ourselves is important if we are to learn the most from each event. Without treating ourselves with the proper style, learning is blocked out by defensiveness or self-condemnation. Basic to our attitude toward ourselves must be gentleness, love, and crystal-clear honesty. But as our mood changes, so must our approach when looking at a situation to use it for good information about ourselves.

For instance, if we are stressed-out, the approach must be one of gentle intrigue: "Let's see what is happening so we can break things down a bit." In the case of anxiety, a soothing desire to hear ourselves out is appropriate. When we are moody, bored, defeated, or passive, we need to be passionate and encouraging—maybe we even need to give ourselves a little push to get out of ourselves and reach out to others so we remember to be more grateful for what we have.

As well as style of approach, a greater way to move toward clarity is to punch holes in the darkness of negative situations. This can be done by *increasing our awareness of the positive*. Too often when we seek greater self-awareness for psychological and/or spiritual reasons we raise the volume of our own sensitivity to ourselves. The goal is to bring into consciousness those preconscious games that are hidden from our everyday awareness. To do this we look at the times we get upset and say to ourselves, "Aha, here is another area where I am holding on!" We also may seek to see in sharper relief those times when we are angry, cowardly, filled with blame for others, pompous, proud, in denial of our own part in making difficulties for ourselves and others, and when we excuse or minimize the negative things we have done and continue to do in life.

Seeing one's faults in light of day is good. It helps us do something about them. A problem arises though when we allow these "clouds" in our life to gather and we let them join so we no longer see the positive achievements and gains we have made. To counter this, as we would do in mentoring others, we must also do the same with ourselves. In other words, we need to recall to mind where we have had the ability to change for the better and take care not to dismiss these successes if we are failing in our efforts now. When we have raised the volume against the defensiveness in our lives then we can recall where we have experienced the freedom to act and break through our habits, fear, and petty addictions.

Toughness is also important in gaining clarity. All of the techniques in the world designed to make change and self-awareness easier won't make seeing things clearly and acting on our insights easy. We must seek to toughen ourselves up so we can face the difficult insights about ourselves in the same way that we embrace the progress.

One spiritual master said to his disciple, "Tell me what you see in me and, in turn, I will tell you what I see in you." His disciple said to him, "You are a good person but a little harsh." In response, the master said, "You are good but your spirit is not tough enough yet." The obvious goal: Build a good and tough spirit in looking at our own foibles, escapes, and excuses.

A *willingness to deal with unpleasant specifics* in our life also enhances the possibility we will be more and more honest with ourselves. Too often in life our journey stays on the level of "the general" where it can't touch us where we live in daily life. Yet that is where change must happen. If we wish to be an author but don't write, how will our dream become true? If we say we desire to be more compassionate but treat those who live and work with us awfully, then of what real value is our commitment? Bringing the responsibilities home so we can see clearly our role in the difficulty and act to change it literally means to face what is in front of us. When we do this the rest of life will follow suit.

However, once again, all of the steps pointed out must be done without vindictiveness toward the self. The part of us that needs attention must be seen as a prodigal child welcomed home to be understood and helped to change.

Seed of Change #5

Being honest with ourselves requires us to: look with compassion at our style of interactions with others; have an appreciation of the progress we have already made as well as the areas of growth which need attention; and be in touch with ourselves so we don't avoid seeing and correcting specific lacks in ourselves.

6. Change Begins in Front of You

By softening your style with the
people you interact with each day

Future dramatic changes in life may seem romantic but in reality they are not worth very much. New freedom and real change begins *in the now*, in front of us with the people with whom we live, travel, and work. Any alteration of lifestyle or change of habit begins here. On New Year's Eve it is easy to make promises for the new year. It is easy to behave a certain way with people who don't know us. However, the sometimes difficult but simple soil in which to plant seeds of true change is our own "inter and intrapersonal neighborhood": the relationships with our family, friends, coworkers—even, maybe especially, the relationship with ourselves.

Once we have decided on an attitude or style of behavior we would like to alter in ourselves, we need to ask how we would practice it. In my own life, I have been told and believe it to be true that my greatest gift in life is "passion." I am a naturally energetic and enthusiastic person. This is great but as in all gifts, it has its downside. If I'm not careful the beautiful passion can turn into my being intrusive, overwhelming—being a real annoyance to people. Rather than letting them share their gifts, take their seats at the organization or family table so they can flourish too, I take all the seats.

I have all the answers. The result is not very pleasant. People eventually react negatively. Then I become defensive, while failing to see my dominant destructive role in the interactions. The thought that arises at such times is: "Well, that's the last time I try to help them!" or "I was only trying to give them my ideas. They can just do it any way they want now. I'm done helping!"

Another equally unclear approach is when I try to cover my own negative feelings with a veneer of chronic niceness. My attitude hasn't changed ("I'm right. They're ungrateful and ignorant!") but I feel I should be "more charitable." Naturally, this approach ends in failure, too. People see I'm being pedantic and controlling and react either overtly or passive aggressively by indirectly showing their anger by undercutting my efforts. Then I get angry because they are not doing what I wanted them to do. I don't even see that I am a fake and a manipulator. The result is bad feelings all around.

There is another way, though, and the good news is that all of the power to make this change is in me and the best place to try it is right in my daily circumstances. By looking at my own passion I can ask the questions: How can I share it in a way that it doesn't edge out other people? The response for me now—because we must be flexible enough to find and employ new ideas as time/circumstances change—is to seed gentleness in my own heart. The lesson: *By softening our greatest talent, we allow it to be our greatest gift.*

Think about any style of those you know and you will find this is true. There is the creative, relational executive who drives people crazy because he never makes a deadline and is so scattered. Should he give up his talents? No. But if he would soften his style with a little more organization, he would be an awesome leader. The helpful cousin who takes on too much and expects others to express their gratefulness, then becomes resentful when she feels unappreciated or overworked—once again, should this person stop being helpful? No. But by looking at her motivation and proactively limiting others when they ask too much, she will truly be a grateful giver.

Softening our central style is a key change which opens the door to being more balanced. With such balance, less defensive energy is wasted and more is available for growth and further change. Also, the best place to practice is right in front of us; the ideal people with whom to hone our style are those who know us best. Our daily routine can then be an actual "course" in uncovering greater inner freedom in ourselves. Isn't that wonderful?

Seed of Change #6

As well as practicing new behaviors (based on what we have learned about ourselves through reflection, study, and reviewing the helpful reactions of others) with people we don't know, we must practice them every day with our hardest—and potentially most helpful—audience: the people with whom we live and work each day.

7. Making Time to Change

So we don't continue to just fill
our life with mindless activities

Religious literature, especially that of Buddhism and classic Christian writings, suggests we keep our own death before our eyes. An image of life used in Tibet is that of getting into a boat which is about to go out to sea and sink! "How morbid!" most people would respond today. But since it's a fact that we are going to die, isn't it silly not to appreciate our limits so our life can be rich within its boundaries?

Such a recognition would make the time of our death a surprise but not a shock. And besides the religious value of such preparation, it would also help us make time to think about how we want to live our life, and what we want to change *now*, while we still have life in us.

I can always tell when I or others of my acquaintance are avoiding this much needed space for self-reflection because of the (in)famous defensive phrase which is invariably used: "I'm too busy to take out time to reflect, renew, and change myself!"

We seem to always have time to worry, preoccupy ourselves, eat or drink too much, scheme against the other person, have an affair, watch hours of mindless television, try to control/please others, complain endlessly about our world, or work impulsively. Yet we say we don't have time to reflect on who we are and where we are going. Crazy? Yes, crazy! But aren't most of us like this? The question is, do we want to remain a part of the irrational "crowd"?

One of the most deceptive ways people avoid being reflective is to claim that being busy is practical and necessary, whereas reflecting on life is a luxury, navelgazing for the rich and indolent. To them I say: How practical is it to run as fast as you can without taking time to pick up your head and see where you are going? Do we wait until we are ready to die to ascertain whether the life we have lived was what we wanted? Or, do we do it every day, week, month, and year?

So, one of the essential rules of inner freedom and change is to *ensure you have time to reflect on your day, week, month, year, and life as it develops.* This is not a luxury but one of the most practical things you and I can do. Otherwise, the only time we make decisions or vows, if we can even call them that, is on New Year's eve, when we are in a bad way, or feeling hurt. The reality though, is that decisions to change such as these guarantee no profound change at all. *I'll never do that again!* more often than not will just turn into doing the same thing over and a feeling of being trapped in old behavior. Change, like anything good, needs time to ponder and plan. It's the practical thing to do. And so, if we are serious about being free from excessive influence by our past experience or our present situation, and wish to be free to constantly change and grow, we need to prioritize reflective time. In this way, quiet moments become the valuable place we know we can enter for reappraisal and new learning about ourselves and our surroundings.

Seed of Change #7

Time for reflection at the start and end of each day, week, month, and year are priorities for people who wish to be truly free.

8. Your Private Place

Where you go to hear
helpful information

As a rule we rarely take advantage of one of the best
places to learn what needs attention and change or
what is blocking our growth. Because this "place" is so
precious and powerful, people often speak about it with
a sense of awe or, at the very least, wistfully. Yet it is
available to all of us every day if we are able to remove
the resistances to going there. The place? It is the inner
self that is welcomed home when we are able to find
silence and, if possible, solitude in our lives.

The fact that we expend so much energy convincing ourselves and others that we can't go there
demonstrates, albeit in a paradoxically negative way,
how much powerful information is available for us
in that place. Valuable self-knowledge often comes to
the surface when we take a few moments to quiet our
hearts and experience life rather than distance ourselves
from it through analysis and excessive, seemingly
endless activity.

The first step toward overcoming resistance to
enter this place of awe, challenge, and information is
honesty. We must be honest enough with ourselves to
admit that we don't really want to go there. Otherwise,
we will be doomed to continue to undermine and avoid
being silent and alone in reflection and meditation,
while deluding ourselves with excuses like "I don't have
the time." If we want something bad enough we can

always find the time. And since the silence and solitude provide real fuel for change, we need to recognize the resistances to it, see what they tell us about why we don't want to quiet ourselves, and then answer these objections clearly and honestly so we can fully reap the rewards of this private place.

The *first objection* is: "When I quiet down and try to enjoy the silence, all I do is hear the noise of my thoughts and worries. So I know I'm not made for meditation or reflection." This is a typical objection of beginners. It needs to be handled, otherwise we will quit after a couple of minutes, no matter how many times we try.

The reality is that most of us hear noise in our minds all day long. When we sit in silence the first important bit of information we get is to learn how preoccupied we are with so many things. Knowing this is helpful because it:

§ *Helps us let the static expend itself. (Given a chance, after a while our mind calms down);*

§ *Gives us some indication of the type of worries we have about which we feel helpless or anxious. (We get a chance to hear what we are continually thinking);*

§ *Prepares us to empty our minds so we can breathe deeply, relax, and experience "the now" rather than always being caught in the past or preoccupied with the future.*

So, expecting the noise and letting it move through us are two ways we can meet the objection that we are not suited or able to quietly reflect or meditate. The reality we must remember is: Many people with our personality type have found meditation wonderfully helpful. It is not just a certain type of person.

A *second objection* is: "Meditation or reflection is too hard and alien. I'm not a yogi and have found meditation or even quiet prayer uncomfortable." The response to this is simple:

§ *Find a quiet place (alone if possible).*

§ *Sit up straight.*

§ *Close your eyes or keep them slightly open looking a few feet in front of you.*

§ *Count slow, naturally exhaled breaths from one to four and repeat the process.*

§ *Relax and let stray thoughts move through you like a slow-moving train, repeating themes; observe objectively then let them go. . . .*

§ *Experience living in the now.*

A *third objection* comes in the form of a question: "What will this time do for me? I'm a busy person and time is too precious for me to deal with impractical exercises." There are many responses to this. For our purposes here—namely, the desire to change, grow, and be more free—the following are especially relevant:

§ *When we are quiet we are able to experience all of the pulls, anxieties, and conditioned responses we have going on all day but may fail to notice. So, at the very least it informs us of the nature of the blocks we have to feeling at ease, flexible, open, and ready to change when necessary.*

§ *Not only will we be able to see what absorbs us but how things we didn't realize have become our most important reference point or center of psychological/spiritual gravity.*

§ *Once we have this information we can take note of it and reflect on it mentally, in journaling, or with a mentor during other periods outside of the quiet time.*

§ *Also, the peaceful times when we sit and reflect physically stop us from running, running, running, without taking a breath, to experience what it means to be alive and, in turn in the process, ask ourselves if that is where we want to focus our lives.*

If it sounds like I'm putting great emphasis on quiet time, I am. I have found if we give some space to ourselves and try not to judge ourselves/others harshly, avoid panicking or trying to immediately solve a problem, but instead calm ourselves down, we will learn not to jump to quick conclusions; our usual ways of doing business (our programming) will not take hold. This will allow our habits to loosen their hold on us so we can see life—including ourselves—differently.

When people do express their gratitude for having put into place taking at least two minutes a day for quiet reflection first thing in the morning, they often then extend it to twenty minutes. Then they try to find another ten minutes during the day to reconnect with the experience and find another few minutes in the evening to become tranquil, give closure, and release the day before they go to sleep.

In guiding others toward using meditation as a building block to enable change, one of the other things I also notice is that it loosens people up throughout their whole day—not just during the reflection period. The more we allow our thoughts to inform, rather than frighten, depress, or anger us, the less we are grasped by our thinking and interpretations. We are not in a vise but are instead free to use our power of observation, analysis, and curiosity to help us learn valuable lessons about life. Meditation not only frees us to be open during the period of reflection, it also produces an attitude that makes us less defensive and more intrigued with stumbles as well as triumphs. It can positively contaminate our day!

Seed of Change #8

Quiet time is encouraged when we realize deep in our hearts that these sacred, precious periods in our life help us: (1) see the noisy worries that are driving our lives toward sadness, grasping, and anxiety; and (2) enable us to appreciate what it is like to stop running and enjoy being "in the now."

9. Real Preparation for Change

Careful reflection

An excellent way to avoid real change is to lead a life dedicated to "pseudo-preparedness." There are those who make a god out of discernment. To call such persons procrastinators is an understatement. By the time they've decided what changes to make in this phase of their life . . . the phase has ended!

Instead, making true preparation to change involves:

1. *Finding time to reflect;*

2. *Selecting meaningful events in our day and life to reflect upon;*

3. *Entering those events by reliving them in our minds;*

4. *Given our desires, goals, and philosophy of life, to learn what we can from these events;*

5. *Enlivening the learning through action.*

Time: A little time is needed to reflect on one's day. If we rush through life without thought we will know it. One sign we are doing this is the statement: "Where did the time go?" When our life is passing like a blur it doesn't mean we live very *active* lives. What it does show is that we are leading *busy* lives. The difference between active and busy is the former includes reflection and is directed, whereas the busy life feels out of control and does not seem purposeful or meaningful.

Select: To make our reflection useful and not just a time to preoccupy ourselves, worry, or let our mind wander, we should pick out *specific* events or interactions during the day that caused a significant reaction.

Enter: Then we should put ourselves back into the events so we can relive them. This time as we experience it we can observe our reactions, note them, and see what themes or understanding we can glean. (Remember, don't *blame* others or *condemn* self, just neutrally observe and seek to analyze.)

Learn: Given what we understand and what our core beliefs (psychological or spiritual) are about life, what did we learn from this reflection? Often when we have values, we can see how we followed those values or ignored them.

Action: Finally, learning is only important when it changes the way we live. How we will act on our new learning is essential. And it can't be action that is immature such as making the vow, *I'll never trust him again!* when you feel a person has let you down. Instead, using the example just cited, you must see what about the interaction led you to be naïve and put more trust in a certain person than he/she could bear. So, in other words, action must be based on insight that we have about our *own* behavior, beliefs, and thoughts. Otherwise, the results will be just a sophisticated form of pouting, projecting, and avoidance of self-understanding.

Seed of Change #9

Each day reflect, select, enter, learn, and act as part of the process of understanding the specific interactions of our life as well as our perception, style of reactions, and beliefs about the people/events that we encounter.

10. What Have We Got?

The inestimable value of a notebook, a few
moments, and some pertinent jottings

If I asked someone, "Do you have a few moments each
day to change your life?" I feel confident the answer
would be "Certainly!" But if I asked if she/he would be
willing to do a little daily journaling, the answer would
be, "Oh, I don't have the time for that!" Yet taking notes
on our life is one of the most valuable and rewarding
aspects of a program of change for persons intrigued
with where they are bound and where they are free.

When we sit down quietly at the end of a day with
a pen and a notebook we are backing away from the
bustle of life in general and taking stock of our life in
particular. We may note stories we've heard, quotes we
have read, or record experiences which struck us.
Journaling is an ideal way to record what we have learned
from our reflections. Moreover, some other good things
about having a notebook or folder in which we put our
daily or weekly reflections are:

> The activity of . . . writing is one that removes us
> from a world of competition and comparisons.
> Journaling is by and for the one who "journals";

> Because we often forget fleeting but significant
> feelings and thoughts, journaling provides a clear,
> detailed record while the impressions are clear;

Moving into the future requires that we know what we have done in the past so we can employ learning in the present. This is difficult when we have no record of our progress—or lack of it;

Writing allows us to see what we are thinking and feeling, so it encourages us to summarize and internalize our understandings better. (One member of the U.S. Congress was asked what he felt was the greatest challenge facing the U.S. Senate today, and he said: "Not enough time to think." Journaling is another way to provide us with this time for reflection); and

. . . writing helps us to see connections and themes so we can learn from the deep center of ourselves that can come to the fore during the quiet process of recollections and writing.[6]

The most common resistances to journaling that I have heard are:

§ *I don't have the time.*

§ *I'm not a writer.*

§ *I don't know what to write.*

§ *What if someone sees what I've written?*

§ *Why would I write down what I already know?*

All of these questions and statements are connected to a lack of familiarity with the process of journaling. It can take as little as a few minutes, it is just for your own use so it doesn't require special skills, and you need only record what happened during the day as well as the feelings and thoughts you had.

No one need ever see what you've written, and in writing down the day's experiences as well as your reaction, many surprises are in store. Not only will you often uncover things that you would not have known had you not engaged in journaling, but you will also find that when you don't make a record, much of what happened will be lost to memory.

Fran Dorff, the author of *Simply Soulstirring* (cited in the recommended bibliography), also notes that writing is a way of meditating, becoming quiet, internalizing what we've learned about ourselves, becoming attentive, and remembering our lives in a way that encourages greater integration of those parts of ourselves that have been temporarily lost but need attention if we are to be able to change and move on in life.

Writing freely what comes to mind helps us see information that is vital for change. Inner connections, deeply felt reactions, and inspirations which come up in journaling might be missed, and then they would keep us from seeing beliefs and emotions that would either block or facilitate change. You can't deal with what you don't know. So writing helps to bring things to the surface that we might otherwise miss or not have access to.

Writing also quiets us down at the end of a day. "Going inward" helps us shed the events and distortions of the day so we can settle down. Journaling allows the confusion in life to settle so we can let our heart become more quiet and our mind deepen in reflection.

Another benefit is that by writing we can reexamine our thinking and what we may have said during the day. Journaling not only provides a record but in the process of writing we are putting down in concrete ways corrections made and feelings felt for us to see and read again.

In writing we are also forced to focus our attention on the specifics in our lives. Rather than thinking in generalities and living in the specifics as Alfred North Whitehead notes most people do, we will think as we live and learn—i.e., from the real issues, challenges, and interactions we have each day. Change is possible only when we encounter what has daily meaning for us. Vows made in the general don't stray into the practical heart of our lives. Instead, they are well-meant wishes which are relegated to fantasy rather than standing as guideposts for new realities.

Journaling also stirs up thoughts of the past, *our* past. Powerful memories are important to tap into because *the only memory that holds dangerous power to prevent change is the one repressed (unconsciously forgotten).* Themes in our lives extend from the past to the present. In writing about the memories that surface we have a chance to welcome them home for understanding and release. Otherwise, our attitude will not be open to change but stuck in past situations no longer relevant today, and the problem is that we will never know that this is what is occurring.

Seed of Change #10

Journaling a little each day so we can have time by ourselves to note the themes, joys, and challenges of our day is a simple, very effective way to record the flow of our life.

11. Pacing

How fast is fast?

A colleague of mine always seems in a rush. Walking across campus she looks a lot like a gargoyle on a skateboard. The upper part of her body seems anxious that it's going to be late. The lower part seems like a pouting, lagging child being dragged along.

Speed is funny. Sometimes a desire for quick results only delays progress further. You can be moving quickly, it's true, but you may be going in the wrong direction! In the end, frustration may be paradoxically increased by going faster rather than be reduced by it because we will be moving away rather than toward our desired goal.

In psychotherapy if the patient is bored, the pace of the sessions is too slow; if the patient is anxious, the pace is fast. The same can be said of our lives. Some people seem to vacillate between boredom and feeling overwhelmed because they can't seem to find an optimal rate of change or openness to new, possibly disturbing information about themselves which if seen would free them up. In such cases, people open up, then clam up. It is very frustrating.

In the spiritual life, patience and courage are recommended so we neither avoid challenges nor demand instant results. *Festina lente* in Latin means "make haste slowly." When walking quickly during a storm, a disciple was reminded by his master that it was raining where they were going as well as where they were. Speed itself solves nothing.

The number of changes can also be a problem. In counseling, people are often cautioned not to change everything at once. By changing one thing we can see the impact and have the energy to do it carefully, then we can regroup to take the next step.

Progress is often based on incremental change and the results produced. We take what we know and make it work for us. In the process of doing this, new steps become known.

Progress is also encouraged when we recognize and remember those areas of our life where we are accomplished and free. Discouragement comes when we lose sight of these places of advancement and see ourselves and our efforts all through the lens of the failures we encounter. And so, pacing allows us to learn from change, not lose sight of successes we have, and not be completely set back by what failures we encounter.

Seed of Change #11

Pace the actions in your life in a way that you avoid either going so fast that you become overwhelmed—too anxious at one extreme or bored and stagnant at the other.

12. Letting Go

Instead of grasping

So much energy is spent holding onto things that it is no wonder that people feel too exhausted to become involved in a program of change. Change takes energy, openness, and honesty. And, once again, to be honest, really honest with ourselves, requires us to realize that in so many subtle ways we aren't very candid and clear in our self-analysis. As a result, rather than knowing when we are grasping, instead of enjoying life, we stay in the dark.

There are many good things: health, wealth, success, friends, feeling physically attractive. To desire and enjoy them is wonderful. Yet to be dependent upon them and anxious all the time about losing them is not good. In our hearts we must be free to appreciate and enjoy all that we have without falling prey to spending much of our time and energy trying to secure them so they will never feel lost.

To do this, people feel, is "only being practical." But in reality it is crazy! If we stopped for a few minutes to reflect on our own and others' experiences we would see this to be true. There are people who are in ill health, poor, unsuccessful by worldly standards, appear to have few friends, and may not be physically attractive. Yet they are happy. There are also people—including ourselves at times—who seem to have so much and they are not as happy as they could be. Why? Because people who are truly happy have learned to be free to change and enjoy everything that is before them whereas others have centered in on certain things that they feel are the only things/persons that will make them happy. So, unfortunately, when changes take place in their possessions, as they surely will, they then will become unhappy.

Subtle addictions to things and people do this to us. While we hold on to what and who we feel will make us happy, we are not loving, free, changing people. Consequently, unhappiness, control, security, and fear become our concern. All our energy goes into this and not into being open to change.

Recently, I was giving a workshop to mentors interested in helping others renew their psychological and spiritual lives by being open to change. The first message I gave them is that the greatest gift they can offer others is the gentle, interpersonal space for this to take place. To do this they must be willing to see where their "holding-on energy" is being spent.

To soften them up to seeing these areas, I offered several prediscover caveats to help reduce the resistance to letting go:

1. *Anything discovered does not have to be changed immediately;*

2. *No area should be condemned as holding on— just neutrally observed as if it were happening to someone else;*

3. *No area should be defended—no one is criticizing or attacking, just observing where energy is being spent;*

4. *Observations—even disturbing ones—should be embraced as a wonderful treasure trove of information;*

5. *After each period of observation, the areas of concern should be written down so some record is kept of this discovery.*

With these provisions in mind, I then offered a principle: *Where there is energy (positive or negative) there is usually grasping and/or fear.* When the smoke of a strong reaction is present, the fire of desire is also usually present and we need to know what it is. Otherwise, rather than our passions being good energy, they may be products of unexamined attachments.

Once we understand this, we can then look at broad areas of potential unfreedom that remain hidden under a veneer of so-called likes, goods, and styles of living. For example:

Appearance: *Everyone likes to look good but how much energy should we spend toward the effort, and what are our anxieties with respect to weight, hair (dyeing or grooming it, growing a beard), clothes . . . ?*

Health: *Taking care of oneself is a beautiful way to demonstrate self-respect and value. So, if a* *person eats too much or too little, takes drugs (including unnecessary medicine), abuses alcohol, doesn't even take a walk for exercise, then there is a problem here. The opposite is also true. Some people drive the others in their house to distraction based on their dietary needs, make exercise a religion, or are so concerned about not gaining weight that they are not attentive or relaxed about themselves but preoccupied and practically anorexic.*

Image: *Wanting to know how we are coming across is fine. However, once again, if there are inordinate concerns about being appreciated, liked, seen as helpful, intelligent, or in need of inordinate attention, then there is a problem.*

Control: *It is good to feel one has the freedom to have some control over one's destiny and to have a positive impact on others. Yet as in the other sample areas cited, this too can be an area where we wish too much control. The irony is we often have the opposite impact when too much energy is expended here. By being so concerned about being in charge of our own life, we fail to take enough risks that in the end would give us more security. Those who invested all their money in bonds and government securities in the 1960s, '70s, '80s, and '90s lost retirement earning power in comparison with those who put some or all of their money into stocks in established companies. Paradoxically,* *parents who are too controlling with their children and employers who are too overbearing with their employees usually breed rebellion in the very persons they wish to influence.*

So, in varied aspects of our lives, we need to ask a simple question: *When do I get upset or feel the happiest?* How we answer the question will lead to wonderful information about our values and preferences. It will also guide us to those places where we have become frozen, excluding other possibilities for ourselves and others. Once again: feeling joy is wonderful; being upset on occasion is natural—the problem is not with the emotion or experience but in not knowing why we really felt this way. By questioning ourselves further, there is so much helpful information for us to mine.

Seed of Change #12

Whenever you react with great emotion, see it as a wonderful red flag pointing to what you are attached to (i.e., image, power, security . . .) and giving up inner freedom because of this attitude.

13. Bringing Role Models Closer

So they can help you

There is a tendency to keep potential role models at a distance. The media colludes in this regard. It first elevates people that are very different from us. Then investigative reporters dig up every little bit of dirt they can to show us that the idols they provided for us have clay feet. This provides a see-saw effect on our psyche and discourages our soul. We get a message which is very disheartening: namely, real wisdom figures and truly good persons are rare—if they exist at all!

This message is pure nonsense! Moreover, it is destructive to the natural and needed movement in society to both seek and be mentors. All of us should try to be role models for others—not by being fake or putting on a good face in a particular role, but by being all that we can be. Each day (it is too discouraging if we try to do this for longer periods of time) we need to accept the challenge to be the best we can be at home, in the office . . . even in the grocery store.

Again, by this, I don't mean we should practice "chronic niceness" and put on a plastic smile. Nor do I mean we should seek to be like someone famous or familiar who has a lifestyle or personality that is nothing like ours. What is essential is that we model, while also seeking a role model for ourselves. Our role model should be the kind of person we believe we would look like if we dropped some of our defenses and let our personality flourish.

In therapy patients are able to change partly because the therapist functions at some level as a role model. The patients say to themselves: "I trust that this person, while not perfect, is living in truth, with greater flexibility, and an openness to greater possibility than I am now. I can follow her lead. I can borrow her strength and try, step by step, to risk change, to explore new possibilities."

In spiritual guidance, the role of a sage also is essential. In Christianity it may be the image of Christ, who didn't cling to his divinity so people could see their own humanity and possibility in him. Paul's bold suggestion to put on Christ is truly the will to be free with Christ. In Buddhism and Hinduism it is devotion to a guru (literally meaning "one who removes darkness") and a deep desire to join one's will with that of this spiritual master.

In daily life there are lessons and opportunities like this for all of us. In business there may be a person whom we admire. In our family an older sibling or cousin may have a similar personality style as we do but be more personally integrated. Or, in a well-developed saga or biography, we may see possibilities in others that we wish to follow.

For years I felt a need to be more gentle as a way of softening my passion. In Shirley du Boulay's biography of Bede Griffith, *Beyond the Darkness*, I saw his desire for gentleness was somewhat like mine. I saw that his nature needed toning as mine did and still does. But du Boulay's words about Griffith gave me hope when I read it and continue to do so:

> *It is clear that as a young man Alan was not easy to live with; that the saintly man he was to become was the result of his determination, the fruit of a life of prayer and meditation, rather than the path of a man born with a naturally easy temperament. The search for holiness, the journey on which he was already embarking, is a hard road. If he sometimes overrode the needs of his companions, it was the blindness brought on by the intensity of his own struggle and he certainly paid for it in the remorse that later swept over him. Much later Hugh summed up the way Alan had been and the man he became in a single phrase: "He is much more now a pervasive light than a consuming flame."* [7]

One of the big elements of change, then, is to seek out role models whom we can emulate rather than keep at a distance. To increase the chance that this will happen, we need to find ones that are right for us at this point in our lives.

Role models vary from person to person. One person may seek someone who is inspirational. For another, the primary valued trait is the ability to be a clear thinker or to have a calm demeanor. However, when we think of role models and our emulating them with respect to the words inner freedom, growth, and change, certain spiritual and psychological talents or gifts are present in some form in all truly healthy role models, no matter what their personality style/background. And so, to know what they are is important. Not only does it help in the choice of a person to emulate, but this is essential to know when we try to develop our own inner freedom. In this way we are able to actively welcome growth and change rather than resist it.

Some of the key talents of a person of inner freedom are:

§ *An ability to let go*

§ *Receptive to new lessons*

§ *Countercultural, but not self-righteous*

§ *Intrigue with one's own emotional flashing lights*

§ *Disgust with samsara (the endless wheel of suffering that comes from grasping and attachments) and bad habits*

§ *Curious, not judgmental*

§ *Values experience*

§ *Recognizes danger of preferences which prevent experiencing new gifts in life*

§ *Awake to present; is mindful*

§ *Appreciates quiet meditation*

§ *Generous and alive*

§ *Learns, reflects, and applies wisdom in daily life*

§ *Rests lightly in life*

§ *Knows the difference between freedom to be versus freedom to choose*

Seed of Change #13

Seek and emulate role models who will inspire, challenge, encourage, and guide you in the quest for greater inner freedom.

14. More Helpful Voices

Both outside and inside

Meaningful change doesn't happen when we act alone. We need helpful voices. Some of them may be the role models we just reflected on, others may not. As a matter of fact, they may not always be people. *Good reading* may educate and inspire us. Biographies, for instance, provide us with opportunities to see how others cope, what failures to avoid, and what dreams to embrace.

Music may ease our spirit and set the mood for quieting the day's anxiety, and meditation. Energetic songs may accompany us when we are in a creative place. Lyrics that are meaningful can also support us so we don't feel alone or lost.

Works of art can be friends as well. Museums are sacred places of silence and possibility. When we surround ourselves with beauty it fills us and calls us to appreciate life more.

Nature is another kind of friend. The songs we hear in the morning amongst the trees. The quiet, cheery welcome of a garden. The movement of the skies we see when lying on our backs at the beach. A swim in the ocean. A mist lifting off the mountains. Standing by a lively stream. Watching the playfulness of animals. All these things have the possibility to inspire us.

People, of course, are very important voices of encouragement and challenging thoughts as well. Just as we seek out music, art, and nature to help us live life in a way in which we are open to the motivation for change and growth that enters our life each day, we need to find a circle of friends who will form a milieu to inspire continued development and the embrace of real freedom.

Likewise, just as we avoid music, art, and places in nature that bring us down rather than open us up, the same discerning eyes are needed with respect to friends. Change for the better is facilitated by friends who:

§ *Challenge*

§ *Inspire*

§ *Support*

§ *Help us laugh at ourselves*

§ *Educate*

§ *Listen*

§ *Call us to greatness*

But no friend is perfect. We cannot expect that one or two people will be able to represent all of the "voices" we need to support us. We need a broad range of talented people to bring out at least four "voices" in our own inner life. In this way we can truly reflect on our emotions, thoughts, and beliefs, and take action in ways which open, rather than close, us up.

Change requires us to be an *evaluator* (Did I do what I said I would about taking certain steps in my life?), a *visionary* (What do I do next?), an *organizer*

(How do I plan and enact my steps of change?), and an *artist* (What creative ways can I improve my life and inner spirit?). All of these "voices" of change within us are given life when we have friends for the journey who remind us that these ways of viewing ourselves are important.

Seed of Change #14

Seek to have a balanced group of friends who will encourage you to evaluate your past actions and attitudes, help you have a meaningful view of the future, be able to structure what you wish to achieve, and be creative enough to not be captured by any present approach to the extent that it cannot be altered when necessary.

15. Real Generosity

A sign that good attitudinal
change has taken place

There is an unusual and powerful connection between change and generosity. A *mitzvot* (stringless gift) is associated with a person who is wealthy in spirit, whereas persons who give with expressed or hidden expectations are often seen as manipulators and strangely needy.

Buddhism speaks constantly and explicitly about the interrelatedness between spiritual wisdom and true compassion. Christianity echoes this in its theology and Islam stresses it in the importance of hospitality.

When we view successful people in Twelve Step programs, who are they? They are the sponsors. People not only faithful to their own one-day-at-a-time journey, but those who also walk with many others.

Although there are times when we must focus primarily on our own journey, these are limited and rare. All good change is not just for us. It is ultimately for *others*. Even the famous fourth-century hermit Anthony left his cave after battling his demons in order to be a service to people of the day.

A simple act like losing weight may seem the sensible thing to do to be more attractive. Similarly, giving up cigarettes, eating good food, and not overindulging in alcohol may on first blush appear to be a healthy act only for the person involved. But the absence of secondary smoke, the positive behavior changes that ceasing alcohol abuse often causes, and the new energy one has to be of help when eating healthily do benefit others. There are no truly private sins or graces; all we do affects others in some way.

So even taking out time to meditate in silence and solitude is really a gift to others as well. The changes it causes are obviously beneficial to the meditator, but think of what often happens to the person who then impacts others. A contemplative person often is:

§ *Less grasping, freer, more generous, and easier to be around;*

§ *Calmer, understanding, and open to the gifts of others;*

§ *More gentle and humorous.*

So, even the most private of beneficial changes—becoming more contemplative—turns into a real gift to others *if* it truly is a change for the better.

Change to benefit only ourselves doesn't benefit us at the core of our being. If change doesn't fill us up allowing us to be less addicted, bound, fearful, anxious, stressful, and ungrateful for each moment, then how is this change really contributing to our own well-being? Possessing something we want and making changes to obtain it may give us a passing feeling of pleasure or security, but there will be little peace or joy in it if there isn't a true benefit to someone else. Moreover, the change probably won't last if we feel it only to be of use to ourselves. Going back to the issue of giving up something that is harming us is a good illustration of this reality.

Seed of Change #15

Recognize that a generous encouraging person truly exemplifies inner freedom. Those who wish to be free only for themselves and not so they can be a gentle compassionate person to others as well, will never find the sense of peace and change they wish.

16. A Little Effort

Not magic or too much work

Being open enough to change is difficult for some people from the start because of two extreme, erroneous beliefs. One is that change happens magically for some. The other common fallacy is that change is really impossible, too much work. The reality is that seeding one's inner freedom is neither: It is possible but it also takes some discipline and a bit of work.

Those who feel freedom is a gift given to people who don't understand that each person can find greater openness and peace if they are willing to do something to gain it. That is what this book and the ones in the bibliography are all about: namely, gradual, quiet change through simple, manageable steps that alter our attitude toward life.

Simple Changes is based on the belief that increasing freedom is like driving a car at night. You see a bit, move a bit further, and so on. By taking to heart lesson by lesson and spending the energy needed to appreciate, remember, and act upon each one, in the end great changes can be the result. It is the positive domino effect.

The "little effort" involved usually centers on risk. To become freer we must risk leaving an old style of behaving and a somewhat comfortable image of self behind. Yet when we realize we have less to lose than if we try to stay the same in a changing, challenging world, then we see that the effort and motivation needed are both worth it.

All of us are somewhat fearful of the unknown, how others will react, what we might lose, or the way we might feel if we do something wrong or silly. However, when we put these worries up against the joy of not only achieving greater freedom but also being involved in the excitement of the very process of seeking openness and change each day, how can anxiety win out?

Yet even taking small steps requires a little effort. While inner freedom is not magic or too difficult, some work and risk are needed. People who don't want to make the effort don't want to see this. One accomplished person shared with me that his cousin's wife always used to say to him: "Everything you touch turns to gold."

He confided in me that: "She didn't want to acknowledge how hard I worked, the risks I took, or my failures along the road. She discounted or ignored the necessary pain I experienced. She preferred instead to see it as magic, but I assure you I didn't fall into it. It took steady effort and reasonable risk at each step of the way."

He is right. A life of inner freedom is both possible *and* takes effort and risk. The first section of this book has offered some of the ways to turn the possible into the actual. It has also pointed to ways to seed our attitude so it is more open to live less tied down by the chains of habit. In this way we are more apt to see possibilities where before we feared change. The next two sections will build on this by answering common questions asked of clinical psychologists and spiritual sages about how to open our minds and soften our souls to new, more satisfying ways of thinking, believing, and acting in life.

Seed of Change #16

Living a life of inner freedom is neither easy nor impossible. It takes a little discipline, courage, risk, and hard work.

II
So What Else Would You Like to Know about Resolving Psychological Resistance to Growth and Change?

~ Commonly Asked Questions about Discovering Greater Inner Freedom ~

So What Else Would You Like to Know about Resolving Psychological Resistance to Growth and Change?

~ Commonly Asked Questions about Discovering Greater Inner Freedom ~

Having completed the book's reflections on ways to encourage change, freedom, and growth, there are probably other questions you have. A bibliography is provided at the end of the book for additional and more in-depth reading; to fill in the gaps, review, and expand on the reflections offered. In addition, following are practical responses to questions commonly asked about why people resist change and how they can begin to remove inner blocks (resistances) to growth. At the very least, I think it will serve to reinforce much of what has been noted in the book and clear up some other questions the reflections might have prompted.

What is the psychological essence of inner freedom?

Don't prejudge. Picasso used to lament that it was a shame we couldn't pluck out our brain and just use our eyes. Too often past experience fastens a biased perception onto what we encounter. This prevents us from seeing things simply as they are.

Instead, we see things as we wish them to be, as we fear they might be, or as we feel they should be. Wishes, fears, and shoulds cloud our eyes and prevent clarity.

Are there signs I should be aware of that I'm not being open to the help I've sought from others to help me grow or change?

Classic signs that we are resisting help from others that would enable us to be more open to change include:

§ *Frequently arguing or taking issue with suggestions being offered*

§ *Holding back on sharing information because of shame or lack of trust*

§ *Making excuses for not doing the agreed-upon tasks between sessions/meetings with your growth/ change consultant/mentor*

§ *Complaining that real progress is too difficult for you to accomplish*

§ *Blaming others for your lack of advancement*

§ *Focusing on the differences between you and your mentor as a way of excusing your lack of compliance with suggestions offered for consideration*

§ *Monopolizing time together to the extent that the other person can't get in a word*

§ *Being late or missing sessions*

§ *Not taking responsibility for bringing information to the meeting but expecting that the consultant will provide the agenda*

§ *Repeated, extended silent periods*

Are there ever times when I disagree with someone guiding me, and it is not resistance to change but a healthy difference?

Yes. When you have different philosophies with respect to what one's goals should be in life. The situation in which this most frequently happens is in work situations when you are being given feedback by someone who is, in the organizational chart, responsible for helping you grow professionally. For instance, in an end-of-the-year evaluation, a supervisor said: "You are so talented I'm surprised you are not more ambitious." After reflecting on this feedback, the man replied to his boss: "Oh, I think I'm very, very ambitious. However, I think we may be ambitious for different things." When the supervisor asked him to explain and heard what the man meant by this, both realized true differences in what was being valued rather than the presence of resistance to risking and expending energy to move ahead.

If I work with someone (a supervisor, mentor, therapist, spiritual guide . . .), what are some of the ways I can *reduce* my resistance to the change and growth I seek?

If you are willing to consult someone to help you change and grow you have already overcome the first block which most people never get beyond: namely, the simple admission that you need assistance. You can't do it alone. Once you've taken that step, some additional ways you can take advantage of the consultant you have is to follow some simple, but often not easy, guidelines:

- § *Be honest.*

- § *Avoid second-guessing or preparing answers while your consultant is speaking. Instead, listen carefully.*

- § *Achieve as much clarity as possible as to what your goals are in seeking this relationship; ensure you both are in agreement regarding the objectives.*

- § *Recognize that though the principles of change, growth, and achieving greater freedom in life are usually surprisingly simple, they take work.*

Is there a style of thinking I should seek to incorporate which encourages growth, change, and the search for freedom?

Yes. If you see yourself as an adventurer, or part of a group of psychological and spiritual pioneers, as people in the forefront of creative business like inventor Edison and Buckminster Fuller, you will get excited about the very process of change. Even failures will teach and intrigue you. The important attitude that encourages this type of thinking is: I will enjoy the process or journey toward greater freedom, change, and enlightenment and not just focus on the end result.

What about the other side of the coin? What tip-offs do I have that my thinking is resisting change by being defeatist, inappropriate, or negative, and how can I short-circuit self-defeating thinking?

Real change becomes difficult when we are ambushed by negative beliefs and unhelpful attitudes. All real growth requires that we surface and answer the messages that have held us back—maybe even for years!

The best way to see this is to catch yourself in the act of making broad negative statements and answer them:

Answer the thought: "I'm a failure" with "I didn't succeed this time. What can I learn from what happened?"

Respond to: "I guess I am just not meant to change or grow" with "What happened today that I found discouraging?" "Why am I so discouraged?" and "Did I set my goals in a way that they were meant to deflate rather than to challenge me?"

Replace "Changing is impossible! It's just too hard" with "Progress does take some work but each step is manageable."

And instead of "My life is hopeless; I need to win the lottery," remember that "When things don't go our way, it may feel hopeless, but when we break things down and take it step-by-step, there's reason for hope."

People say you can also use humor to dispute irrational thinking that's holding you back. I'm a fairly serious person, though, so what can I do to tease myself so I can see how ridiculous my beliefs or reactions are?

One way is to *exaggerate* something to the point of the absurd. You can tell yourself when you fail that: "It is the worst thing that has ever happened in the world. No one in the world has ever made a mistake like this!"

What are some of the major thoughts/beliefs people use to defeat themselves?

If I had a list I might be more sensitive to some of them when they appear so I could dispute them.

How to Defeat Yourself Effectively and Make Yourself Miserable No Matter How Good Your Life Is

§ *Don't ever seek to fully understand your problem; it might help.*

§ *Use projection; Don't take the blame . . . it might lead to change!*

§ *Believe you are incapable of having an impact on your own life.*

§ *Tell yourself work is unnecessary for change.*

§ *Never admit you need help—especially when lost or confused.*

§ *Don't pay attention to instructions.*

§ *Whenever possible refute, argue, and be sarcastic.*

§ *Say "yes" but really mean "no."*

§ *Delay, block . . . be passive aggressive.*

§ *Use up all your energy in fantasy instead of being a visionary who saves some to act upon the dreams to make them come true.*

§ *Avoid self-discipline.*

§ *Always change guilt into shame. (Say to yourself: I didn't make a mistake . . . I am one!)*

§ *Stay loyal to the negative place that your family and society gave you.*

§ *Waste your money.*

§ *Increase your debt.*

§ *Swallow ads that make you seek approval and spend money.*

§ *Don't look for hidden agendas.*

§ *Never look at anything you've done wrong to understand it better—only to make yourself feel worse.*

§ *Search for clues from family, friends, and acquaintances for approval and then do all you can to please them.*

§ *Medicate self with alcohol, work, etc.*

§ *Learn how to threaten yourself! (i.e., Tell yourself if you don't succeed you will be miserable.)*

§ *Avoid the pleasure of the process of seeking change so you discourage yourself.*

§ *Don't preach the value of living with inner freedom—it may cause you to believe it yourself.*

§ *Don't laugh at self—it may lead to gaining perspective.*

§ *Avoid positive imagery and good role models.*

§ *Believe problems and successes are magical and don't require a little discipline.*

§ *Don't challenge general negative views of others or yourself.*

§ *Convince yourself that it is terrible, terrible, terrible to give something up.*

§ *Hear praise in a whisper and criticism as thunder.*

What are some essential psychological points to remember and reflect upon which will help me overcome resistances to growth and change?

In addition to what has been covered thus far and the psychological value of the spiritual lessons included in the next section, the following points may be helpful to ponder:

§ *Psychological maturity is an invitation to be more honest with ourselves concerning our gifts and our growing edges.*

§ *Simple changes that are profound involve letting go of old beliefs and ideas that are no longer true or may have never been valid—they only seemed so because we've held onto them for so long.*

§ *Counselors and therapists offer unconditional regard so people can feel safe enough to explore themselves without fear of judgment or rejection; enlightenment occurs when we can also do this for ourselves.*

§ *"Musts," "oughts," and "shoulds" evidence different lacks of freedom in discovering life on our own.*

§ *True maturity and health relies on a person having periods of quiet where they can relax rather than panic, cooly assess rather than judge, and understand rather than impulsively jump to emotion-laden conclusions.*

§ *All sound treatment and self-awareness involves stepping back from hurts, needs, angers, worries, and fears to see what perception is propelling them in these negative directions.*

§ *Clarity is often not possible without having a sense of humor.*

§ *The psychological journey to inner freedom involves recognizing, understanding, and removing the supposed hidden value from those habits, conditioning, and attachments we feel are so indispensable to our being happy.*

§ *Losing our defenses does not mean losing our natural style of interacting with others; instead, having healthier motivations for what we do makes the style everyone knows more encouraging to others to be freely themselves as well.*

Reflecting on the above can also be aided by taking the following strong, exciting, and energetic steps to get rid of stubborn, self-defeating behavior:

a) *Become determined not to catastrophize your failures or have unrealistic expectations for yourself.*

b) *Monitor your reaction to see where you are needlessly looking for something to make yourself miserable.*

c) *Enjoy the process of change in itself.*

d) *Model and teach others to behave in the compassionate, positive way you are also practicing in your own life.*

e) *Constantly tease yourself when you get cranky, pout, or are annoyed with yourself and others.*

f) *Uncover your negative thinking and dispute it in the same way you would help others to do so—but do it with even greater energy and fearlessness.*

g) *Practice the productive psychological ways you have learned to improve the tenor of your life and enjoy your efforts at it—because whether or not you fail or succeed in an individual attempt at something, you are still living a more fascinating and full life for having tried to dismantle your habits/rigidity in order to live with greater freedom.*

III

Dialogue with the Sages:
Spiritual Approaches to "Softening the Soul"

III

Dialogue with the Sages: Spiritual Approaches to "Softening the Soul"

Jewish rebbes, Christian mystics, Taoist sages, Hindu gurus, Buddhist rinpoches, Muslim imams, and Russian startsi have passed down great wisdom through the ages. People wishing to find ways to till the soil of their lives so they may have greater freedom to change and deepen themselves have sought their guidance. In the following section I have joined some of their voices in response to some of the more common questions about living a life marked by greater flexibility, openness, and freedom. To build on and amplify these comments, a selected bibliography is provided at the end of this book. The spirituality books listed there and the books they in turn cite should provide added clarity to what is offered here.

Spirituality teaches us that change is not just enacted by going through a series of acts. As important as action is, it is the *attitude*, way of perceiving, that determines the depth and extent of one's freedom to change. Also, spirituality literature always involves "the other." Whether this "other" is God or a fellow traveller to whom we must be compassionate, listen, or follow, change is never viewed as something closed in a vacuum.

Whether or not you are religious, I think you will find the following comments adopted from contemporary and ancient spiritual wisdom literature of much benefit and encouragement. They have been designed to be of service to a wide audience.

How do spiritual guides view resistance to change?

Classic and contemporary spirituality literature views resistance to change as something natural. Phrases like "harden not your hearts," "people prefer the darkness to the light," and "remove the beam from your own eye instead of focusing on the splinter in someone else's" point to this. Contemporary Zen masters teach that if you feel you are already free, you are lost. Tibetan Buddhist rinpoches see life as an opportunity to move through layers of resistance and even subtler forms of attachment, fear, and grasping as a way of finding more and more freedom. The question is not whether there are blocks, "sins," or areas of holding on to illusion/status quo, but *where* are they now.

Since there are so many obstacles to inner freedom and change that are present even in highly motivated and enlightened people, how can we avoid discouragement—especially if we feel as if we are only beginners?

You should always seek to see yourself as a beginner because we literally always are! We are always beginning the next phase of our life, peeling away resistance after resistance, seeing more and more light. Disappointment is a sign that our proud, fearful ego, which has inflated itself with a false sense of accomplishment, is being unmasked and made to feel helpless. The first appropriate response to disappointment is to laugh at ourselves—or, more accurately, at the part of us that thinks it is a god who has achieved nirvana. After that, we need to be intrigued at what caused the disappointment and what this can teach us. Sometimes the disappointment is triggered by how someone reacts or by something they say to us. The Dalai Lama would remind us that these people can be our best teachers if we are able to learn from both their criticism and the emotional responses they trigger in us.

What would be an example of something someone who doesn't like me could teach me that would help me be freer and able to change?

There are certain images we like to project at work and in social settings. The energy it takes to keep up these efforts to impress or deceive people is enormous. Moreover, they can cause quite a bit of conflict when we are with people from different areas of our life since we may wear different masks to impress people in certain ways depending on the setting. Although their motivation is not good, people who point out our charlatan tendencies help us to see that we are not being real. Also, the "unrequested prophets," our family, circle of friends, and work setting, may indicate where we are falling short as well. Once we drop the masks or see faults, we have the energy and direction to improve ourselves.

Can't we be angry for good reasons that have nothing to do with us?

Rarely. Even anger at injustice usually contains good information about our own defenses, insecurities, and the games we play to control our surroundings and maintain a certain image/status quo. An example from my own life was when a new supervisor wanted to radically change the way a project I was working on should operate. My reaction was: *He* is awful! I was obsessed by how to stop him and save what I felt was good. Finally, with the help of spiritual guidance I was taught to see my obsessions at retaining control. It was both freeing and enlightening. Metaphorically, it was like finding myself in a musty cellar surrounded by old useless possessions that I thought I had gotten rid of long before. To see these possessions (defenses, negative personality traits, etc.) anew helped me to see what needed to be faced in me, not the supervisor. Then, with a heightened sense of self-understanding, I could approach the situation with a greater sense of neutrality and openness.

You make it sound like failure, defect, anger, and sadness are good. Are you saying we should seek such things?

No, of course not. To do so would be masochistic or an unusually dramatic gesture. However, when such experiences come our way, isn't it foolish to just feel the emotional pain and not learn everything we can from it?

Is everything my fault? Shouldn't other people change, too? Are there no times when I should request change of others?

Whether other people change is ultimately up to them. When we change is up to us. The first step is always to look at our feelings, thinking, beliefs, expectations, and actions. If we do this, with a spirit of true exploration rather than blame-seeking (i.e., whose fault is it?), we will discover a great deal about ourselves. With this knowledge we can suggest that others change. However, if we react when we feel negatively then it will only cause more harm—even if the person/situation changes.

To get through the challenges and discouragements, are there some simple offers I can remember?

First, recall how far you've already come in your desire to progress. Too often when we fail at something we believe all of our success up to this point was a sham. This belief is false; don't believe it. *Second,* when we don't succeed we tend to ignore those areas of our life that are good, filled with joy, and in which we have made strides. Remember these when times are not good. *Third,* move away from being oriented too much toward the end result and become more involved in and enjoy the process. We will always have tasks uncompleted and goals unfulfilled; not to enjoy the journey of growth and change in itself is foolish.

In the search to be more open and deeper as a person I have great goals for myself. They are what motivate me to overcome resistance to change. Yet when I read the spirituality material it seems to say: "Don't expect anything." This seems ridiculous. If I didn't expect anything, then why would I seek to change or grow? I might as well just stay as I am.

You're right to expect that good will result from your commitment to being a person who values freedom, openness, spiritual growth, a commitment to what is true and good, and a desire to be compassionate to others. However, it is in the *specifics* of how this will come about that predictions and expectations can be fatal to what you may experience. To hope that a vacation will be rewarding is understandable. Yet to see it as a complete waste if it rains is the foolish result of expecting that holidays are only good if it is sunny. Expectation deprives us of seeing so much in persons, situations, and life in general. We get chained to the expectations and concepts, and in the process ruin the surprises and fullness of the experience in which we are involved. Though it is not always the case, this is the reason why some people grow from painful experiences and others just become bitter. Those who grow are open to receive new gifts amidst the pain; others close themselves up and cling to the suffering.

Meditation is recommended by most spiritual figures. What is the connection between it and spiritual growth or the ability to change?

A time for meditation offers an opportunity to let the dust of the day settle. It also moves us away from nostalgia or preoccupation with the future and allows us to experience the present. Meditation also allows us to break away from the constant compulsion to act, control, do, compete, compare, and win. It gets us in touch with our mortality, the impermanence of life, and the gift of every day. We can then bring this experience of "looseness" from the chains of compulsiveness into our day so we are not merely swept along by unexamined beliefs or driven by subtle addiction/motivations.

If meditation can help people experience life, appraise the way they have been leading it, and help them to be clearer, why don't more of us do it?

There are many reasons for this. One of the main ones is the feeling that nothing is accomplished in meditation; real change takes action! However, if you run in the wrong direction in life, what good is that? Another obstacle is the claim that it's too hard or there isn't enough time. How hard can it be to sit up straight, breathe, and relax? People often respond by saying that they don't relax. Meditation just gives them the time to worry or ruminate. The reality, though, is that thoughts coming to us during meditation are running around in our heads all the time anyway. Meditation helps us to learn what such messages are. Why should we have the puppeteer's hands hidden in our life? Meditation lets us know what is really driving us. If we let these thoughts move through us without indulging them, then two things will happen: We learn about ourselves and they will eventually quiet down so we can be at rest and be one with life. If we are religious, we can also see it as a time to rest in God and be grateful for the gift of life. Another indirect benefit will also be the way it calms us down so others can approach us more easily. Meditation is, in a word, *amazing*.

All religions seem to make a strong connection between spiritual development and compassion. I understand that I should be of service to others, but what does this have to do with change in me? If I want to be a better salesperson or lose weight, isn't that strictly a personal goal?

The spirituality underlying most major religions would claim that what you call "a strictly personal goal" is very egotistical. If personal change isn't also connected with a desire to be more compassionate, then not only will it not make other people happy, in the end the change will not benefit you as a person. From this vantage point, hedonism is seen as very foolish because the very person who seeks pleasure is ruining the great pleasure and enlightenment that comes from being compassionate. Moreover, I have found being compassionate also teaches us a great deal about ourselves and helps deepen the development and accelerate the growth we desire. For instance, if I want to be a better listener, the more I am available to others, the better I can hone such a skill. If I wish to be less influenced by others and be more spontaneously myself, by interacting with others and offering them a gentle space to be themselves, a lot can be achieved. For one, I can see areas that I still need to work on (i.e., discovering areas I am resistant about in dealing with others). For another, I can see the joy in others when they respond positively and call me to continue my effort.

Such an attitude would radically alter how I look at personal and professional improvement, wouldn't it?

Yes, it would. If you saw an unbreakable bond between your own quest for freedom, insight, and wisdom, and the opportunity to be of greater service to others, your relationship with all of your life's work would change. If you saw everything you did on the job, in social situations, and even in meditation as opportunities to grow for the benefit of others, the pain of being overly involved in your own image and ego would be diminished. You would experience a new freedom and the adventure of change would be one filled with intrigue and excitement, rather than dread. When personal development and service to others form a "circle of grace," then the moodiness and anxiety that come from selfish over-involvement with self diminishes.

When I get frustrated or sad about how foolish I've been in life, is there anything I can do? Sometimes I feel I've wasted so much time being cautious or afraid to change.

Being sad is all right. It's a recognition that holding on to a pattern has caused suffering. Such sadness is part of loosening the bonds to a habit, idea, or belief that has held you back. It is appropriate grief. However, it is important to use this sadness beneficially and not to dwell on it so future movement is not possible. When this occurs, it is depression (which requires treatment) or extreme self-pity. Drawing strength from the sadness can occur when we recognize that even a minute of true enlightenment if it is grasped and lived out can make the life left in you—no matter how little it may be—precious and good. Sponsors in Twelve Step programs demonstrate this when they greet a returning alcoholic who went back to drinking after years of sobriety. Instead of dwelling on the devastation they say: "Well, you are here *now*." The "now" is a beautiful antidote to despair.

Sometimes I feel if I can just get over the problems I am experiencing now in life (i.e., money, my son's illness, my sister's divorce, my husband's anger, drinking too much . . .) everything will be fine. Yet I know there will be other problems—an endless list of them. How can I keep hope alive feeling this way?

These "feelings" are really thoughts about life based on the belief: "All will be well once I conquer my problems." However, the problems we must face are like *koans* (life puzzles) that can't be answered or conquered. Instead, they should help us to let go of the way we are approaching life to seek new, more creative ones. For instance, if a person is diagnosed with a terminal illness, he must let go of the idea he will live "forever" (another twenty to forty years) and ask what is quality living in the present. It is when we refuse to let go of our old ideas that we are in trouble.

Meditation helps in this regard because it often loosens up the way we view things. In the few quiet moments of reflection, habits are temporarily broken and our crazy compulsions and worries rise to the surface and drive through our minds like a train if we don't indulge them but just take notice with objectivity.

If we could bring such a way of viewing our life in meditation into our daily life it would be wonderful. We would enjoy and see clearly our present life in a way that we wouldn't be captured by fears, oughts, shoulds, needs, and rules. Life would be fresh, clear, and clean. When we live this way we are always a student of life and don't have to pump ourselves up because we feel we must be a proud teacher. The ordinariness and humility we feel in meditation when we are quiet and alone without any props can also be present in life if we let it. This then leads to experiencing the wonder of wisdom that arises when knowledge is joined with humility.

I know there are no set rules to follow in the spiritual life that will lead to guaranteed freedom. To think that is to exchange one set of rigid thinking for another. However, are there guidelines that would help me be more open so I am less captured by my own narrow perceptions and more welcoming to the wisdom that the world teaches if only I have the heart to see?

You have already embraced one of the guidelines: namely, to recognize that you are already blind to some extent. It is when we believe we are fully free that we are bound by the unrealized beliefs and dogmas that we swallowed long ago and haven't questioned since because we didn't realize we were being driven by them. Some other simple tenets of inner freedom you might find helpful are:

§ *Although truth may cause initial pain or discomfort, in the end it can be our dearest friend.*

§ *Clarity is the way to meet this friend called "truth."*

§ *Fighting to overcome resistances and conquer passions only strengthens them; befriending them we can find out what they promise so we can gently let them know that they can't deliver.*

§ *Being in the now and meeting both the peaceful and the painful, the familiar and unfamiliar, leads to an acceptance of all realities and the following of what is good.*

§ Real "ego compassion"—rather than "superego compassion" based on duty/guilt—connects us with others in a way that fosters integration within us as well.

§ Spiritual disciplines should include offering a gentle space to others, finding quiet honest space within yourself, and receiving guidance from others so both spaces remain pure of grasping and gain.

§ Facing our fears, doubts, boredom, anxieties, anger, charlatanism, and manipulative nature doesn't require much courage when we have humility.

§ Meditation is made up of a little technique and a lot of gentle love.

§ Sadness may come in the silence because that is when this hidden teacher may feel welcome to show her helpful face to remind us that we are holding onto something less than the truth (God).

§ Once you let the pain of an interpersonal encounter wash over and away from you, what is left is a clean truth about yourself that a less relaxed encounter could not produce in a million years.

§ Acknowledge easily and openly both what you're praised and condemned for, and where there was once negative passion will be new wisdom and the continued freedom only humility can bring.

§ Strong emotions are always the smoke of the fire of attachment.

§ *A beautiful sunny morning and a relaxing rainy afternoon remind us that love is around us and that the hurt, doubt, and resentment we have are little parts of our life that need to be released.*

§ *Life is no longer small and unrewarding when we get excited about how we can grow spiritually and be naturally compassionate.*

§ *Flowing with life doesn't stop pain; nothing can do that. Yet it does lessen unnecessary suffering, teach us new lessons, and help us to see the value of patience for new openings. As Thomas Merton says: "Courage comes and goes; hold on for the next supply."*

§ *Spirituality is not designed to make us special. True ordinariness is tangible holiness.*

§ *Lessons in freedom are like a train we are taking on a holiday. Riding itself should be a joy, but not to get off and enjoy your destination is very silly.*

§ *Every period in our life brings new gifts. If we use old techniques and attitudes fail to change, we won't be able to open them.*

§ *Memories are good when they remind us that in some unique, possible, unforeseen way, "all will be well" no matter what happens.*

§ *Persons who really love inner freedom demonstrate it by being open to seeing specific truths about themselves without resentment, hostility, or fear.*

§ *Being able to enjoy life as it is given takes practice; whereas thinking wistfully about life is easy.*

§ *Spiritual persons enjoy life's daily wealth while those around them dream of silly things like wealth, fame, power, and others finding them attractive.*

§ *Those who respect everyone have a wealth of spiritual teachers.*

§ *Anthony de Mello used to tell people: "It is easier to put on slippers than to carpet the whole of the earth." Perspective that comes with spiritual wisdom prevents us from entering "the carpeting business" in life.*

§ *Embarrassment, failure, and awkwardness are the salvific handlers of God's grace.*

§ *What people call "happiness" is really a passing high, after which you will have a corresponding low.*

§ *Our concept of God often prevents us from having the inner freedom to experience God in so many wonderful ways.*

§ *One of the greatest ways you can gift yourself is to observe yourself with interest but not judgment.*

§ *Being free often requires that we forgo pleasing both living and dead family members and friends.*

§ *Take from every role model something to practice in daily life.*

§ *Real role models live what they teach.*

§ *While we need to be open to all people, we must develop and nurture a circle of friends who will inspire and challenge us.*

§ *If we wish to be free in spirit only for ourselves, then we have failed already; if we wish to be free for others, too, our compassionate purpose will purify us.*

§ *The easiest route to appreciating attachments, seeing our grasping nature, and knowing the truth is the recognition of our feelings.*

Reflecting slowly on those of the above lessons that strike you as particularly helpful can further soften your soul so it welcomes freedom and allows you to see changes that are necessary for you at this time.

A Question of Inner Freedom:
An Epilogue

This book has addressed the central question: "What can I do to gain greater inner freedom in my life so that needed personal and professional changes can take place when the time is right?" In answering this question, other questions were posed. This was done so that seeing, understanding, and resolving our inner resistances to growth and change would become more possible.

Among the questions explicitly and implicitly asked as a way to raise our awareness of the blocks in our life were:

In addition to motivation, what other steps do we need to take to gain greater inner freedom?

How do I make more "space" within myself by recognizing and dropping expensive defenses that cost so much psychological energy?

Am I willing to question myself further so I can see my own role in my problems?

When I speak about changing, am I open to address not just the painful parts of my life but also the comfortable parts that may be holding me back as well?

Do I look so directly at my habits, addictions, stresses, games, fears, and anxieties that I am disgusted enough to let go of ingrained styles of perceiving, understanding, and reflecting?

Do I avoid change because of the fear of: (a) seeing my role in problems; (b) not having the comfort of projecting blame but having to take personal responsibility; (c) dealing with negative reactions of others to my healthy change; and (d) the pain I will feel knowing I could have changed earlier in life but didn't?

When I get emotional, the first reaction is to blame others or condemn myself; am I willing to then take a step back and look at it objectively to see what I can do to gain knowledge about myself and the interaction so even failures become "enlightening defeats"?

How can I let irritating events and worries teach me about my attachments, needs, image, and fears?

Are we sensitive to the dangers of arrogance (projection) and ignorance (self-condemnation) when we are involved in self-awareness so that a spirit of intrigue can prevail?

Do we view ourselves as "psychological and spiritual detectives" when we look at our emotions, thoughts, and beliefs?

When we look at our style of interacting with life, do we: (a) take care not to minimize how far we've grown; (b) truly value the positive gifts we have;

(c) seek to be touched enough to be honest about our defensiveness; (d) reflect on specific events so we don't avoid learning by being too vague/global and (e) take some practical steps/actions based on what we have learned about ourselves?

Based on the insights we have received, are we willing to practice new behaviors with the people with whom we live and work?

Do we value inner freedom enough to take out quiet time for reflection each day?

Do we remind ourselves of the value of meditation (i.e., helps us see the worrisome "noise" in our minds, brings us into "the now," etc.)?

Do we take time in the evening to "take notes on our life" by jotting down reflections on the feelings, thoughts, beliefs, and behaviors that we experienced during the day?

How do we understand the notion of "pacing ourselves" with respect to making changes in our life?

What are the ways we can encourage a process of "letting go" in our lives?

Who are our role models, and how do we allow them to inspire and guide us?

Who are the friends in our life who challenge, inspire, support, tease, educate, listen, and call us to greatness?

Why are generosity and compassion two important traits of a person with inner freedom?

What are classic signs that I am not being open to new knowledge and, instead, being defensive?

Am I willing to do the work that change requires, or do I still feel somehow it should happen more easily and miraculously?

Do I seek to see when I am involved in self-talk that contains broad, negative, self-defeating statements and dispute them with more realistic thinking?

Can I try to make friends with my resistances each day by: seeing them as natural; valuing what they can teach me; and facing them directly with intrigue rather than fear or discouragement?

Are we humble and confident enough to see ourselves as beginners so the need to prop our image doesn't destroy our freedom, ordinariness, and openness?

Do we see what sadness, anger, and anxiety can teach us so we don't just have suffering without also learning something wonderful from the experience?

By dealing with these questions, the atmosphere of our inner life changes. We look for awe rather than success. We are more gratified by knowledge than self-satisfied by building up our image or public persona. It's not that we don't feel the pain or rebuff, losses, failures, or unachieved goals. However, we use this pain to deepen our wisdom about ourselves and the life-given realities and true limits of human existence. And so, unnecessary suffering is lessened, the energy it takes to be defensive and protect ourselves is freed up for growth, and we live with greater peace and joy even amidst life's ups and downs.

All of the information in this book, of course, is only a beginning, an encouragement. Yet by reading, rereading, absorbing, reflecting, and sharing with close friends the simple principles and questions in this book, it can provide a basis for a way of life that is never dull, always enlightening, and results in making the most of "the now" you live in each day. Absorbing and quietly (gradually and without fanfare) incorporating key concepts into our attitude and way of viewing the world can make all the difference in how we live. All it takes is a little time, work, and some *simple changes*.

Appendix I

A Month of Change:
An "At-Home 30-Day Retreat"

A traditional, recommended way to absorb life's lessons is to take a periodic retreat. Going away for a few days to a month to take time in silence and solitude can be quite nourishing. Using this time to reflect on material you wish to learn and apply is also quite helpful. However, getting away for any length of time is not always possible. Since this is so, the following is an "at-home retreat" comprised of thirty reflections.

One way of making use of these reflections is to read one in the morning and then reflect back on it throughout the day. Then in the evening take the time to further incorporate the material into your way of approaching life by noting a personal reflection on the quote in the space provided. Over a period of one month these areas can then be slowly taken to heart and bear good fruit.

Another way of reflecting on the material is by taking a day or weekend of quiet time off by yourself to go through these reflections (as well as the questions just noted in the Epilogue) slowly, while noting your own reaction in the space provided. Whichever approach you prefer, this is an ideal opportunity to spend time with spiritual and psychological lessons that can seed freedom in your life to welcome new change and growth.

Day One: Make space within yourself by psychologically and spiritually "cleaning out" your inner life. To find out what is now filling you with defensiveness, grasping, fear, and anger, take note of when you are emotional and see what in *you* is causing this reaction.

Day Two: When you react negatively be careful of the dangers of arrogance (projecting all the blame on others) and ignorance (condemning yourself). Instead, be intrigued by the silly habits and erroneous beliefs which have reinforced such a way of thinking, feeling, and acting on your part. A spirit of *intrigue* is the key to greater self-awareness and excitement about growth and change.

Day Three: Blaming others for your problems may initially feel good. However, when we give away the blame, we also give away the power to change. After all, if it is everyone else's fault, then for change to take place, we need to change *them*. But when we get away from blame and are intrigued with (but not involved in condemnation of) our own role, then we have *the power within us* to make an impact.

Day Four: Get excited about the *process* of change rather than the results. In this way, whether we succeed or fail, we learn and have fun with the process of self-discovery.

Day Five: Find out where the power of annoying events really lies. In other words, ask what sensitive area in *you* is causing such a dramatic reaction.

Day Six: Negative experiences and worries are "helpful pointers" to those areas in our life that we are trying to inordinately control or hold onto. By looking at our daily concerns—especially those that preoccupy us—we can profitably direct our energy to let go, be free, and change.

Day Seven: The two greatest enemies of self-understanding, clarity, growth, and change are *arrogance* (projection) and *ignorance* (self-condemnation). When you pick up feelings of anger, shame, or guilt which signal their presence, try to look at yourself calmly and clearly as if you are viewing someone else so you can retrieve the power present in understanding the situation without injecting condemnation.

Day Eight: In being aware of what we can change for the better, we sometimes forget to see what is already going well. We may also miss appreciating the progress we've already made. Take time to notice your advances so you don't just focus on growth areas and get disappointed.

Day Nine: Toughening our "psychological skin" and not overly personalizing criticism are essential attributes for growth and change. People who are very sensitive have a hard time with self-understanding and feedback because it is too painful. Whether we fit into that category or not, we need to catch ourselves when we get upset and tease ourselves a little bit so we don't get pulled down or have to run away from good knowledge.

Day Ten: Practice looking at *specific* events in the day that evoke dramatic responses. We can learn from them, whereas general feelings or principles don't seem to teach us much. Find individual events, think about them, learn from them, and then enact the learning—that's the way to change. Broad vows or promises do little to move us.

Day Eleven: Any change you wish to make in your life should be practiced with the people you know and love, not just with mere acquaintances. In this way you will have many chances to practice new behavior and be able to get honest feedback about it.

Day Twelve: Any style we have has a productive side as well as an unproductive one. When we are anxious, the negative side appears—i.e., humor can be freeing or it can be dark and demeaning. How and when we use it can teach us about sensitive, blind areas that need more understanding and growth if we are to change.

Day Thirteen: Remember that today you may die. The person you are dealing with may die as well. Knowing this, recalling this frequently, can alter your style of interaction and increase your level of openness.

Day Fourteen: The goal in life is to be actively enjoying and learning from each day so we can share it with others. When we are too busy it means we are preoccupied with life so we can't learn about or share it. Reflecting during the day for a few minutes on what is important can help us keep active but not busy.

Day Fifteen: At least two minutes of silence and solitude to center yourself each morning is a must. (It also gives us a chance to have a sense of what preoccupies us since these thoughts invade the silence at first when we enter silence.) Periods of quiet later in the day break up the compulsive tendency to run to our grave doing "practical, important things" instead of appreciating how precious our life and inner freedom are.

Day Sixteen: True preparation for change in life includes: a little time to reflect; selecting meaningful things in our daily life upon which to reflect; entering those events by reliving them and looking at them without judgment; learning from what we see; enacting the learning in our daily approaches to life. Given the value of this process, how can we incorporate it in our life?

Day Seventeen: Jotting down a few notes at the end of the day is important. Having a notebook in which we comment on feelings, events, thoughts, and desires that stand out is a wonderful way of keeping a record of what is center stage in our life. Reflecting on these notes helps us see what the idols, false beliefs, and areas of defensiveness/"unfreedom" are.

Day Eighteen: Progress doesn't usually occur smoothly or without intermittent failure. Discouragement occurs when we lose sight of advancement and only key in on our mistakes or temporarily return to old, unproductive patterns.

Day Nineteen: Two basic ways to overcome inner resistances to change are by telling yourself:

1. *You don't have to immediately change something you see is blocking you; in this way you don't become overwhelmed by feeling you have to change everything in life as soon as you have an insight.*

2. *All behavior—including negative episodes— should be looked at neutrally, as if it were being done by or happening to someone else. This helps us not to project blame or condemn ourselves as we view what is negative in our life.*

Day Twenty: Areas about which we tend to be defensive and waste beautiful energy that would be available for growth and change are often connected with *images* we wish to project and protect; things/people/events we wish to *control*, and *possessions* we believe we must have to be happy. By searching these areas we can find where we are caught. To do this, ask yourself: When do I get angry, anxious, or upset? In doing this, these areas will come to light to be examined and freed up.

Day Twenty-One: Role models inspire us. Picking ones from your circle of family, friends, coworkers, as well as from books, well-known personalities, and the grand arena of history will enable you to take courage and guidance from an array of "mentors of freedom."

Day Twenty-Two: In our circle of friends, who do we have/need to provide us with challenge, inspiration, support, laughter, education, perspective, and a listening ear? Knowing about the different voices in our life can make all the difference.

Day Twenty-Three: Persons who have inner freedom and are open are recognizable by their natural generosity. Being less defensive and rigid is reinforced by how compassionate we are able to be with others. Our focus here is not a "superego compassion" driven by duty or guilt, but an "ego compassion" that results in offering ourselves to others because we are no longer fearful or needy.

Day Twenty-Four: When asking for guidance from others, we must be "people without guile." In other words, we need to be honest, avoid second-guessing, seek clarity at all costs, and be willing to do the work that self-understanding requires, because it is well worth the effort.

Day Twenty-Five: As you greet each day, see yourself as "an adventurer" and fill your heart with intrigue about what you will find out about yourself and your world.

Day Twenty-Six: Anytime you feel overwhelmed, fearful, very negative, ask yourself what thoughts and beliefs are driving these reactions, once you have them, before you answer them boldly, positively, and assertively.

Day Twenty-Seven: Start each day by becoming excited that you are "a beginner." Beginners have so many possibilities for discovering new insights about themselves and life. Whereas those who feel accomplished are tied to beliefs about themselves and life that often keep their minds and hearts closed.

Day Twenty-Eight: Meditation is a simple way to soften your soul for insights and changes. Find a corner or room to sit up straight, hands on your lap, eyes slightly open, and breathe in and out naturally. Count from one to four and then repeat again and again for at least two minutes. Let the thoughts that come to you move through you like a train you observe but don't indulge with concentration.

Day Twenty-Nine: Tie self-improvement and compassion together. In this way the danger of overinvolvement with self or burnout will be avoided.

Day Thirty: Loneliness and sadness are feelings that point to losses in life. However, they also help us know where we need to be free and unattached so we can enjoy life and people without being captured by the belief that we can't do without them. If we see this clearly, then when we are with people we can love them more freely and enjoy life more completely as it unfolds in front of us.

Completing "A Month of Change":

"I am still learning." ~ Michelangelo's motto

At the heart of inner freedom is a person who is both open and generous. Each of the previous days' reflections were meant to encourage such a desire for both spiritual wisdom and compassionate nature. What additional and central themes not covered in the reflections do you wish to add here to guide your own specific journey?

(Please write them in the space provided below.)

Appendix II
Some Helpful Books

Brazier, David. *Zen Therapy: Transcending the Sorrows of the Human Mind.* NY: Wiley, 1995.

In this brilliant work of integrating psychotherapeutic principles and methodologies with Zen wisdom, Brazier is not only offering a service to professional clinicians but is also providing a wealth of encouraging information for anyone who wants to face and live life in a joyful, compassionate way. I was grateful for having read this book. It provided me with needed information in framing my self-understanding as well as being useful for my work with others.

Chödrön, Pema. *When Things Fall Apart.* Boston: Shambala, 1997.

This book by an American Buddhist is simple, powerful, and thought provoking. As I read it I thought of the Dalai Lama's beautiful words and his startling ordinariness.

de Mello, Anthony. *Awareness: The Perils and Opportunities of Reality.* NY: Doubleday, 1990; *One Minute Wisdom,* 1986; *The Way to Love,* 1992.

With the exception of my own book, *Living a Gentle, Passionate Life,* the three works above are closer to my philosophy than the other books in this brief bibliography. de Mello beautifully integrates psychology (primarily from both the cognitive and transactional analysis approaches) with Christian and Eastern spirituality. These three works are practical, powerful, and simple to follow; wonderful supports for those wishing to be free, open to change, and interested in psychological/spiritual growth.

Dorff, Francis. *Simply Soulstirring*. Mahway, NJ: Paulist Press, 1998.

This book on journaling is a well-balanced and creative treatment of the subject. Fr. Dorff guides us to enter into solitude and become one with our writing, free of distraction, and open to new wisdom. This treatment of writing as a meditative practice is highly recommended.

Ellis, Albert. *Overcoming Resistance*. NY: Springer, 1985.

This is meant for professional therapists. However, Ellis, a famous—some would say infamous!—rational emotive therapist and founder of this way of viewing human behavior, is straight-forward in his approach. I think most people would enjoy reading his comments and increase their understanding as to why people undermine their own chance to grow, change, and be freer.

Kornfield, Jack. *A Path with Heart*. NY: Boston, 1993.

A book on meditation and inner transformation that indirectly but powerfully addresses our resistance to change, growth, and experiencing inner peace. It is a convincing book for anyone wishing to live a fuller life.

Merton, Thomas. *The Wisdom of the Desert*. NY: New Directions, 1960; and *The Way of Chuang Tzu*, 1965.

Both of these books by the contemplative Thomas Merton will offer insights that are terse and original. They will break up the ground of one's preconceived notions and hidden rules of life so new freedom and clarity are more possible.

Rilke, Maria Rainer. *Letter to a Young Poet*. NY: Norton, 1934.

This classic addresses the need for solitude, courage, perseverance, and honesty in the journey to be what we are all called to be in different ways: a committed artist.

Rinpoche, Sogyal. *The Tibetan Book of Living and Dying.* San Francisco: Harper, 1992; and *Glimpse After Glimpse*, 1995.

The first book listed by Sogyal Rinpoche is a masterpiece on Tibetan Buddhist wisdom. There is so much helpful information on flowing with rather than "grasping" life that I feel it would be very helpful to persons wishing to live a full life— no matter what their religion or whether they are religious at all. The second little book (*Glimpse After Glimpse*) contains reflections based on the first one. It can be used to warm up to the larger volume or as a sense of reflection following a reading of the more comprehensive work, which is how I found it helpful. Sogyal Rinpoche is a true master of the spirit of freedom, spiritual wisdom, and compassion. I loved both these books and reread them often.

Wachtel, Paul L., editor. *Resistance: Psychodynamic and Behavioral Approaches.* NY: Plenum Press, 1982.

Paul Wachtel is the psychologists' psychologist. A fine clinical theorist himself, he has assembled a wonderful array of leading therapists to write about resistance. This book is meant for professional therapists, but for those who wish to see the way "resistance" is viewed from a number of theorists, it is a classic in the field. For the nonprofessional, this will be the most difficult book in the bibliography to comprehend so if some things seem a bit confusing, read on in another chapter since some of the material expects a clinical background.

Wicks, Robert J. *Living a Gentle, Passionate Life.* Mahway, NJ: Paulist Press, 1998.

Of all my books, this one I think is the best written and most helpful. Its emphasis on simple, psychological, spiritual

wisdom makes it a good complementary volume to the book
you have just read. In reaching out to others you may also
find my book on mentoring (*Sharing Wisdom*, New York:
Crossroad, 2000) of interest.

Bibliography Notes

[1] David Chadwick, *Crooked Cucumber*, New York:
Broadway Books, 1999, p.111.

[2] Thomas Merton, *A Vow of Conversation*, New York:
Farrar, Straus and Giroux, 1988, p.161.

[3] Robert F. Rodman, *Keeping Hope Alive*, New York:
Harper and Row, p.5.

[4] Anthony de Mello, *One Minute Wisdom*, New York:
Doubleday, 1985, p.57.

[5] A version of this story originally appeared in my book *Seeds of Sensitivity*, Notre Dame: Ave Maria Press, 1995, p.51.

[6] Robert J. Wicks, *After 50*, Mahwah, New Jersey: Paulist
Press, 1997, p.28.

[7] Shirley du Boulay, *Beyond the Darkness*. New York:
Doubleday, pp.52,53.